The Living Bible Story Book

by KENNETH N. TAYLOR

Illustrated by Richard and Frances Hook

TYNDALE HOUSE
PUBLISHERS, INC.
WHEATON, ILLINOIS

This book is a condensation and revision of
Taylor's Bible Story Book
(© 1970 by Tyndale House Publishers).

Library of Congress Catalog Card Number 40-2307
ISBN 0-8423-2307-4
Revised edition © 1979 by Tyndale House Publishers, Inc.,
Wheaton, Illinois.
All rights reserved.
First printing, August 1979.
Printed in the United States of America.

CONTENTS

I
God Makes a Beautiful World

Long, long ago, long before anyone can remember, God made the world. But it didn't look the way it does now, for there were no people, animals, birds, trees, bushes, or flowers; everything was lonely and dark.

Then God made the light. He said, "Let there be light," and light came. God was pleased with it. He gave the light a name, calling it Day. And when the day was gone and the darkness came again, He called that darkness Night. God did these things on the first day* of creation.

Then God made the sky above the earth; and He gave the sky a name, too, calling it Heaven. God did this on the second day of creation.

Now God said that the waters covering the earth should become oceans and lakes, and the dry land should appear. Then He made the grass grow, and the bushes and trees. All this was on the third day of creation.

On the fourth day God let the sun shine in the daytime, and the moon and stars at night.

On the fifth day He made great sea monsters and all the fish. And He made the birds—some, like the ducks and geese, to fly over the water and swim on it and live near it; and others, like eagles, robins, pigeons, and wrens, to live in the woods and fields.

On the sixth day of creation God made the animals, those that are wild and live out in the forests, such as elephants, lions, tigers, and bears; and those that are tame and useful, such as rabbits, horses, cows, and sheep. And He made the little insects, such as the ants that crawl around on the ground and the little bees that fly from flower to flower.

Then God made a man and named him Adam.

This is how God made him. He took some dust from the ground and formed it into a man's body, and breathed into it, and the man began to breathe and became alive and walked around. And the Lord God planted a beautiful park as a home for the man He had made, calling it the Garden of Eden; in it God planted lovely trees full of delicious fruit for

*Older children and parents should understand that the original word in Hebrew, here translated "day," can also mean "period of time." Some authorities believe each "day" was millions of years long. But no one really knows.

God planted a beautiful park for Adam and Eve

the man to eat. A river flowed through the park and watered it.

God told Adam he could eat any fruit in the garden except the fruit from one tree called the Tree of the Knowledge of Good and Evil. If he took even one bite from that tree's fruit, God said, Adam would begin to die.

Adam was the only person in all the world and he was lonely. God decided it wasn't good for him to be alone, so He made another person to be with Adam and to help him. This is how He did it: He put Adam to sleep; and while he was sleeping, He took one of Adam's ribs and made a woman from it. Then God brought the woman to Adam, and she became his wife. Her name was Eve.

God sent all the animals and birds to Adam so he could give a name to each kind.

Then God looked at all He had made in those six days, and He was very pleased. So the earth and skies and all the plants and animals were finished in six days of creation.

On the seventh day, God rested; so it was a quiet and different day from all the others, a holy day of rest.

QUESTIONS

What was everything like before God created the world?

How did God make Adam?

How did God make Eve?

Why do you think God rested on the seventh day?

What did God tell Adam and Eve not to do?

2
The World's Saddest Day

But there was someone else in the Garden of Eden besides Adam and Eve and God. Satan was there, in the shape of a serpent. Satan is the wicked spirit who tempts us to sin. So now the serpent came to Eve and told her to do something that was wrong. He asked her, "Did God tell you not to eat the fruit of any of the trees in the garden?"

"We can eat any of it except from one tree," she replied. "We can't eat the fruit of the Tree of the Knowledge of Good and Evil, for if we eat it, we will begin to die."

"That's not true!" Satan told her. "It won't hurt you at all! God is just being mean to tell you that! Really it's good and will make you wise!"

Eve should have gone away and not

listened to Satan, but she didn't. Instead, she went over and looked at the tree. It was beautiful! And the fruit looked so good! When she remembered that Satan had said it would make her wise, she took some of the fruit and ate it and gave some to her husband, Adam; and he ate it too.

After they had eaten it they heard a voice calling to them. It was God's voice. But they didn't come; instead, they hid among the trees, for now they were afraid of God. God called to them again.

"Where are you, Adam? Where are you?"

"I'm hiding," Adam finally replied, "for I'm afraid of You."

"Have you eaten the fruit I told you not to?" God asked.

Then Adam began to make excuses and blamed Eve. He said, "The woman You gave me, she gave me some of the fruit and I ate it."

God asked Eve, "What is this you have done?"

"Satan fooled me," she said, "and so I ate some of it."

God was very angry with Adam and Eve and with the serpent. He said that the serpent would be punished by having to crawl on the ground in the dust all its life. He told the woman that when her children were being born she would have sickness and pain. And God sent Adam and Eve out of the beautiful garden and wouldn't let them live there any longer; for if they stayed they might eat fruit from the Tree of Life and live forever. So He sent an angel with a sword made of fire to stop them from ever going back into the garden again.

God told Adam that because he had listened to his wife and eaten the fruit, when the Lord had said not to, the ground would no longer grow lush crops for him as it had in the Garden of Eden; instead, it would grow thorns and thistles. As long as Adam lived, he would have to work hard to get enough food to eat; and when he died, his body would become dust again, like the dust he was made from.

But even though they had sinned, God made a way for Adam and Eve to be saved from punishment after they died. He promised to send a Saviour who would be punished for their sins so that they wouldn't have to be punished. God said that if people would ask God to forgive them and would trust the Saviour to save them, and would try to obey God and be good, God would take them to heaven when they died.

When the Saviour came, he died for Adam and Eve's sins, and for their children's sins too, and also for ours. For we, too, have done bad things and need to be forgiven. That includes you and me and everyone else. We are all sinners. But God forgives us if we ask Him to, because Jesus died to take away our sins.

QUESTIONS

Who else was in the Garden of Eden with Adam and Eve?

Did Adam and Eve obey Satan or God? What was their punishment?

Do we ever feel like hiding from God?

Will God punish us?

3

How Abel Pleased God

After Adam and Eve were sent out of the Garden of Eden, God gave them two sons. The older one was named Cain, the younger one, Abel. When they grew to be young men, Cain became a farmer while Abel was a shepherd with a flock of sheep. They both had wicked hearts like their parents, and they often sinned. But Abel was sorry about his sins and believed the promise God had made to send a Saviour.

One day Abel brought a lamb from his flock and offered it as a gift to God by killing it and burning it on the altar. The altar was a pile of stones which was flat on top. He built a fire on the altar and put the dead lamb in the fire to burn up until only ashes and bones were left. Doing this was called a sacrifice. By giving God his lamb, Abel showed God that he loved Him.

God was pleased that Abel worshipped Him in this way, for the lamb was in many ways like the Saviour God would some day send to die for people's sins. The Saviour would be gentle and patient and innocent like the lamb, and would be killed as a sacrifice just as the lamb was.

But Abel's brother Cain did not turn from his sins or believe God's promise to send a Saviour; and when he brought his offering it was not a lamb, which was what God wanted, but some things from his garden. So God was not pleased with Cain or his offering.

When Cain realized that God wanted a lamb as a sacrifice, and had accepted Abel's sacrifice but not his, he was angry with God. Yet God spoke kindly to him and asked why he was angry. If Cain would bring a lamb, God told him, then God would accept his gift and be pleased with him.

Cain was angry with God but took his anger out on Abel. One day when they were in the field together, Cain killed Abel; and the ground was wet with his blood.

Then God called to Cain, "Where is your brother Abel?"

"How should I know?" Cain an-

Cain kills his brother Abel

swered. "Am I supposed to baby sit my brother?"

But God had seen what Cain did, and now declared that all the rest of his life Cain must wander from place to place as his punishment for killing Abel—always afraid, and with no home to stay in. And when Cain planted a garden, it wouldn't grow well, and briars and weeds would spring up and choke it; or it would have leaves but no fruit; so Cain would hardly have enough to eat.

Cain told God that this punishment was too much, and that everyone who met him would hate him and want to kill him. But God said that anyone who killed Cain would be punished with a very dreadful punishment; for God Himself chose to punish Cain, and no one else was to do it. So God put a mark on Cain. We are not told what sort of mark it was, but it was something other people could see; and when they saw it, they knew he was Cain, and remembered God's command that no one was to kill him.

Adam lived for many years after this. Finally, when he was 930 years old, he died, and his body became dust again as God had said it would, because he ate the forbidden fruit in the Garden of Eden. Nine hundred and thirty years is a very long time for a man to live, but in those days God allowed people to live much longer than now.

During those years Adam and Eve had many children, and the children grew up and had children, and then those children grew up and had children until there were many, many people in the world. One of them was Enoch. The Bible tells us that Enoch walked with God. This means that he loved God and thought about God all the time. It was as though he and God were walking along like friends, with Enoch listening to what God was saying and trying to please Him and obey everything He said.

When Enoch was 365 years old, God did a wonderful thing for him: He took him up to heaven while he was still alive! So Enoch didn't die like other men, for God just took him away to live with Him.

Enoch had a son named Methuselah who lived to be 969 years old. The Bible doesn't mention anyone else who lived to be older than that; so Methuselah is called the oldest man who ever lived.

QUESTIONS

What did Abel offer to God?

How is a sacrificed lamb like Jesus?

Why didn't God want Cain's offering?

Why do you think Cain killed his brother?

Which man in the picture is Cain and which one is Abel?

The oldest man who ever lived

4

Saved from Drowning

As the years went by the world became more and more wicked. People did all kinds of bad things. They didn't want to please God and didn't even try to obey Him. So God was angry with them and said He would punish them by sending a flood to cover the earth with deep water, drowning them all.

But there was one good man whose name was Noah. God loved Noah and told him about the flood He was going to send, so Noah could get ready for it.

God told Noah to build a huge boat as high as a three-story house, filled with many large rooms, and having a long window and a big door in the side. He said that when the boat was finished, Noah and his sons and their wives would live in it and float away safely when the flood came.

God also told him to bring into the boat a father and mother animal of every kind there was, and birds and even insects, so that when the flood came, some of each kind would still be alive; for everything not inside would be drowned.

So Noah began to build the boat.

It took him a long, long time, more than a hundred years; but as you know, at that time men lived much longer than they do now.

Noah did something else, too, besides building the boat—he was a preacher, so he talked to the people about God and warned them about the flood that was going to come because of their sins. But the people didn't believe him and they weren't sorry for their sins. All during those long years while he was building the boat, he heard them say bad things about God, and saw the wicked things they did. He patiently kept on working until at last the boat was finished.

Then God told Noah to bring all his family and the birds and animals into the boat, for in seven days the rain would begin and the flood would come, and everyone outside the boat would be drowned.

So Noah brought his wife and his three sons and their wives into the boat. And he brought in at least two of each kind of animal and bird. These were in pairs, a father and a mother of each kind. We don't know how Noah found all the different animals and birds or how he got them

God saves Noah and every kind of animal

to come into the boat, but they came, for God was helping him. Two of some kinds came and seven of other kinds.

When all were safely inside, God closed the door and locked it.

Seven days later it began to rain; in fact, it poured. It rained without stopping for forty days and forty nights. The rain came down as if it was being poured from great windows in the sky. The creeks, the rivers, and the great oceans all began to rise; and water covered the land. After a while there was so much water all around the boat that it was lifted off the ground. Higher and higher the water rose, with the boat floating on it.

But what about those people who had refused to obey God and wouldn't listen to Noah's warning? They had laughed at Noah for saying there would be a flood; they said Noah was only trying to scare them. But now, too late, they saw that all he had told them was true. Oh, if they could only get into the boat, but now it was too late.

They climbed the highest hills and mountains, but soon the hills and mountains were covered with water, too; and there was nowhere else for them to go. So all the people in the world were drowned except those in the boat. And every animal and bird and insect, except those in the boat, died in the flood, for all the earth was covered with the water. There was no land to be seen anywhere; only the boat could be seen, floating alone upon the water.

God did not forget Noah. All through that dreadful storm He took care of him and of all those who were with him. God kept the boat safe. Finally the rain stopped and the water began to go down again.

After Noah had been in the boat for 150 days, almost half a year, the water had gone down so much that the boat rested on the top of a mountain called Ararat, but Noah and his family stayed inside, for God wasn't ready to let them out yet. Two months later the flood had gone down even more, so that the tops of other mountains could be seen peeping above the water.

Finally the ground was dry again, and God told Noah and his wife and his sons and their wives to come out of the boat and to let out all the animals and birds. At last they could walk around outside.

Then Noah built an altar, as Abel had done, and sacrificed animals and birds upon it to the Lord. This was his way of thanking God for saving him and his family from the flood, though all the other people in the world had drowned.

God promised that He would never send another flood to drown all the people. As proof, He gave Noah a sign—a beautiful rainbow in the sky where Noah could often see it when it rained; and whenever he saw it, he would remember God's promise not to send a flood like that again.

QUESTIONS

Why did God send the flood?

Can you remember what people went into the Ark?

What happened to everyone else?

Do you remember the last time you saw a rainbow?

What can you think about when you see a rainbow?

5

A Huge Tower

Soon after the flood ended, Noah became a grandfather, for God gave children to Noah's sons and their wives. These grandchildren grew up and had children, too, until after a while the world was full of people again.

Don't you suppose these people would be very careful not to make God angry? They knew about the terrible flood and what had happened to all the people before. But no, they didn't care, and kept on doing all sorts of bad things. Perhaps they weren't afraid of God, because of the rainbow and God's promise not to send another flood. But there were many other ways for God to punish them. He could send sickness or war or not enough food, or He might send down fire from heaven to burn them up. But they seemed to forget this; their hearts were bad so they acted just like the people before the flood, and constantly sinned against God.

There was only one language in the world at that time. Today there are hundreds of languages, like English, Spanish, French, and German. (Can you name five more?) But in those days the people all talked alike, so everyone in all the world could understand everyone else!

One day the people said to each other, "Let's build a high tower, as high as heaven!"

So they began to build it. We are not told why they wanted this tower, but probably it was because they were proud and wanted everyone to see how great they were to build such a high tower. But it is sinful to be proud, and God knew what they were thinking.

One day the Lord came down from heaven to see the tower, and He was not happy about it. He decided to stop the people from building it. So He made them begin to speak in different languages! Now they couldn't understand each other! One man would ask another for a hammer, but the other man couldn't understand him! This made them angry with each other, and soon they stopped working and went home.

They didn't even want to live near each other anymore, so all those speaking the same language lived together, and moved away from those who didn't speak their language. That is why different languages are spoken in different parts of the world today.

So the tower, which was called the Tower of Babel, was never finished. The word "Babel" means "mixed up." When people began to talk in different languages and couldn't understand each other anymore, they got all mixed up. That is why the tower was called the Tower of Babel.

QUESTIONS
Did the people try to obey God?
Why did they want to build a tower?
What did God do?

6

The Story of God's Friend

Far away in the land of Ur (or Iraq, as we call it today), there lived a man named Abram. The people of his country worshipped idols made of wood and stone. This was very wrong of them, for God had said that they must worship only Him. God told Abram to go away from people like that and to move to another country.

So Abram left his home and relatives and friends and travelled far away to a distant land with his wife Sarai, his nephew Lot, and his servants. He had never been in that land before, but he believed God would take care of him. Abram was seventy-five years old at that time.

It was a long, hard journey. They had to cross wide rivers and a desert where the country was lonely and wild. Yet God took care of them and brought them safely to the promised land. It was called the land of Canaan. Today we call it Israel.

"I will give all this land to you—this whole country," God told him. "It will belong to you and to your children forever."

Then Abram built an altar and worshipped God by killing an animal and burning it on the altar.

Other people were living there in the land who might have harmed him, but God kept them from doing it. It was a time of famine when Abram arrived. Famine means that the grass and the grain didn't grow well, so the people had little to eat.

Now Abram went away for awhile to still another country called Egypt, and waited until there was more food for them in Israel. Then he and Lot and their families returned to Israel again, and Abram sacrificed to the Lord again by killing a lamb and burning it on the altar.

Soon Abram became very rich and owned many, many cows, goats, and sheep. Lot had many of them too.

But the men who took care of Lot's animals quarreled with the men who took care of Abram's animals. When Abram heard about this, he talked to Lot about it. Do you think Abram said, "This is my land, Lot, and you get out—God has given it to me, and you must move away somewhere else?" No, Abram was very nice to Lot and said, "Let's not have any fighting and quarreling between us."

Then Abram and Lot divided the land. Abram gave Lot first choice, even though he didn't need to—it was his land, for God had given it to him.

Lot chose the very best part of the country, the valley of the Jordan River. One of the cities there was named Sodom. The men of Sodom were very bad, but Lot went to live among them anyway. He was not a bad man himself, for he worshipped God; but he went to live among these wicked men because he thought he would have better pasture for his cattle in their country and that he soon would become rich. He shouldn't have done this, and we will soon see how much trouble it caused.

After Lot had moved away to his new home, the Lord said to Abram, "I will give you all of the good land Lot chose. Lot is living there now, but some day it will all be yours!"

God also said He would give Abram so many children and grandchildren and great-grandchildren that they would become a great nation. That promise has come true and today we call Abram's people the Israelis, or Jews.

QUESTIONS
Why did God want Abram to move?
Why did Abram and Lot divide the land?
Why did Lot choose the Jordan Valley?
Do you think Abram or Lot behaved better?

7
God's Visit with Abraham

One hot day as Abraham was sitting at the entrance of his tent, he looked up to see three men coming toward him.

He ran to meet them and threw himself down in front of them with his face to the ground, for that is the way strangers were welcomed in that land. Abraham invited the men to rest in the shade of a tree while he brought some water to soothe their tired feet. In those days people either went barefoot or wore sandals, so their feet became very dusty. One of the things a friendly man did for his guests was to give them water to wash their feet after a long, hot walk.

Abraham ran to the tent and told Sarah, "Quick, bake some bread." Next he ran out to where the cows were and selected a fat calf to be killed and cooked.

When the meat was ready he set it before the men, with some butter and bread and milk, and they had a picnic beneath the tree while Abraham stood nearby to serve them.

After they had finished eating they started off toward the city of Sodom, and Abraham walked along beside them.

Now I must tell you that these three men were really not men at all. Two of them were angels, we believe, and the other one was God.

Could God look and talk like a man? Yes, several times in the Bible He appeared in the form of a man and talked with someone.

God told Abraham that He had decided to burn up the cities of Sodom and Gomorrah. Why was He going to do this? It was because the people who lived there were so bad. Abraham was very sad when he heard about this, for Sodom was the city where his nephew Lot lived. He was afraid Lot would be burned up too. Abraham talked to God about it.

"Perhaps there are some good people living in the city," he said. "Must they die too?"

God replied that if there were only fifty good people in the entire city, He wouldn't destroy it.

"But perhaps there are only forty-five!" Abraham said.

And God replied, "If there are even ten good people there, I won't destroy it."

Then God went on to Sodom, and Abraham returned to his tent.

That evening Lot was out by the city gate; for in that country the cities had walls around them to keep out enemies, and there were gates in the walls to go in and out.

As Lot was sitting there, suddenly the two angels stood before him. But Lot didn't know they were angels because they looked just like men. They were the same angels who had come with God to Abraham's tent. Lot stood up to meet them and invited them to come to his house to spend the night.

"No," they replied, "we'll just camp out here."

But Lot was afraid of what the bad people of the city might do to them, so he begged them to go home with him. Finally they agreed.

After supper the angels asked him whether he had any other sons or daughters in the city beside those who were with him at home.

"Go and warn them to leave Sodom at once," they told him, "for the Lord is going to destroy this city."

Lot ran quickly to the homes of his married daughters and said to his sons-in-law, "Quick, get your families out of the city, for the Lord is going to destroy it."

But they didn't believe him, and Lot had to come back home without them.

Early the next morning, while it was still dark, the angels said to him, "Leave the city at once, or you will be burned up along with all the other people living here. Take your wife and your two girls and get out right now. *Hurry!*"

"Don't look behind you," they said. "Hurry to the mountains where the fire won't kill you."

But as they were going, Lot's wife looked back toward Sodom, even though the angels had told her not to. She died right there and became a statue of salt.

The sun was just rising when Lot and his two daughters arrived at Zoar.

Then the Lord rained down fire from heaven on Sodom and Gomorrah, completely destroying both cities. All the people in them died, and all the grass and plants and trees were destroyed.

God saved Lot and his two daughters, but Lot lost everything, including all the nice things he took to Sodom when he and Abraham left each other.

Early that morning when Abraham came out of his tent, he saw a great cloud of smoke rising from Sodom and Gomorrah. He knew God hadn't found even ten good people in the entire city of Sodom, for God had promised not to destroy it if He found even that many good people there.

QUESTIONS
Who came and talked to Abraham?
Were all of Lot's family saved?
Why did Lot's wife turn into a statue of salt?

8

Rebekah Says Yes

Abraham was getting very old, and the Lord had blessed him in every way.

At this time God gave Abraham and Sarah a little baby son, just as He had promised them. Abraham named him Isaac, for that is the name God had said to give him.

Abraham was 100 years old when Isaac was born. What a happy day it was!

When Isaac grew up and became a man, he wanted to get married. But his father Abraham didn't want him to marry any of the girls in that country, because they all worshipped idols instead of worshipping God. He wanted Isaac to marry a girl from the country where his relatives lived, where the people obeyed God and didn't worship idols.

But that country was far away. So Abraham called his oldest servant, the one who was in charge of all his business, and asked him to go to that distant land where his relatives lived and

Lot's wife looks back

to bring back a girl for Isaac to marry.

"But what if I can't find a girl who is willing to come so far?" the servant asked.

Abraham told him, "God will send an angel ahead of you to help you find the right girl to come and be Isaac's wife."

So the servant loaded ten of Abraham's camels with beautiful presents and started off.

After many, many days of hard travel he finally arrived at the town where Abraham's relatives lived. He made the camels kneel down by a well that was just outside the city.

It was evening when Abraham's servant arrived at the town, and the girls were all coming out to draw water from the well. As the servant watched them coming, he asked God to help him find the right one to be Isaac's wife.

How could he ever know? This is

Abraham and Sarah waited a long time for their son Isaac

what he decided to do. He would ask one of the girls to give him some water from her pitcher. If she answered him with a smile and said, "Yes, and I will water your camels too," then she would be the one God had chosen to be Isaac's wife. But if she was grouchy and wouldn't give him the water, then she wouldn't be the right one.

While he was still praying, a beautiful girl named Rebekah came, carrying her pitcher on her shoulder; she went down to the well and filled it with water.

The servant ran over to her and said, "Please give me a drink from your pitcher."

"Certainly, sir," she replied, "and I'll water your camels too!"

She let down her pitcher from her shoulder and gave the servant a drink, then ran back to the well and began drawing water for his camels!

After the camels had finished drinking, the man gave Rebekah a gold earring and two gold bracelets. He asked her whose daughter she was and whether there was room at her father's house for him and his men to spend the night. Rebekah told him she was the daughter of Bethuel and that there was plenty of room.

When the servant heard her say she was Bethuel's daughter, he realized that she was a cousin of Isaac's, for Abraham was Bethuel's uncle. He was glad, so he bowed his head and worshipped the Lord, thanking God for helping him find the right girl so quickly.

Rebekah ran home to tell her mother that the men were coming. When her brother Laban heard about it and saw the earring and the brace-

lets, he ran to the well to find the man and to bring him home. After Laban had helped him unload the camels and feed them, it was time for supper, so Laban took Abraham's servant in to meet the family.

But the servant said he couldn't eat until he had told them why he had come to their country. He said that he was Abraham's servant and that the Lord had blessed Abraham and made him very rich. He had silver and gold, flocks and herds, camels and donkeys; God had also given him a son, Isaac, who needed a wife.

He told how he had come to the well that day and had prayed that God would help him find the right girl to be Isaac's wife. He had prayed that if she was the right one she would answer pleasantly when he asked for water. He told them that while he was still praying, Rebekah had arrived. When he had asked her for a drink, she had said, "Of course, and I'll water your camels too!"

Then the servant asked them whether or not they would let Rebekah go with him to marry Isaac. They said yes; since it was the Lord who had brought him to them, Rebekah could go.

When the servant heard this he was very happy and worshipped the Lord. He brought out other beautiful presents—jewels of silver and gold, and beautiful clothing—and gave them to Rebekah. And he gave her mother and her brother presents too.

At last he and his men were ready to eat, and afterwards they stayed at Laban's house all night.

In the morning, Abraham's servant wanted to take Rebekah and leave at once to return to Abraham.

Abraham's servant meets Rebekah by the well

But her mother and brother said, "Let her stay with us a few days at least, and then she may go."

The man begged them not to delay him, for he felt that he should hurry back to his master again.

They said, "We'll call Rebekah and ask her if she is willing to go so soon."

She replied, "Yes, I'll go now."

So they sent her to Isaac and never saw her again, for Isaac's home was hundreds of miles away.

After many long, hot, weary days of camel travel, they came at last to Canaan just as the sun was going down. Isaac had gone out into the field for a walk, to be alone with his thoughts. Perhaps he wondered back and whether God had helped him find a girl to be his wife. What whether the servant would soon be would she be like?

Just then he looked up, and the camels were coming!

When Rebekah saw Isaac walking in the field, she asked the servant who it was, coming to meet them. The servant told her it was Isaac. Then she took a veil and covered her face with it. Isaac brought her into the tent that had been his mother's before she died. And Rebekah became his wife, and he loved her.

QUESTIONS

Why couldn't Isaac marry a girl from his own country?

How did Abraham's servant find the right girl?

Who was she?

Why do you think God answered the servant's prayer so quickly?

Do you think it was hard for Rebekah to go so far away?

9
Joseph's Dreams

One of Jacob's twelve sons was named Joseph. He was the youngest in the family, except for Benjamin.

When Joseph was seventeen years old, he went out into the fields one day to help his ten older brothers who were taking care of the sheep and the goats. But while he was there he saw his brothers do something they should

not have done. That night when he got home, he told his father. This was a good thing to do, for then his father could talk to his brothers about it, so that they would not do it again. But of course his brothers were angry with him for telling on them.

Joseph was his father's favorite son, so his father gave him a present of a beautiful coat. But this made his brothers jealous. From then on they couldn't seem to find one good thing to say about him!

One night Joseph had a strange dream, and the next morning he told his family about it.

"In my dream," he said, "all of us were out in the field tying bundles of grain stalks. Then your bundles stood around mine and bowed to it!"

This dream made his brothers even angrier. They thought Joseph was saying that they should bow to him as though he were their king.

"Do you think you are better than we are?" they demanded.

Then Joseph had another dream. This time he dreamed that the sun, the moon, and the eleven stars all bowed to him. His eleven brothers knew he was talking about them when he talked about the eleven stars bowing to him; and the sun and moon must mean their father and mother. This made them angrier than ever.

When he told his father about the dream, his father scolded him.

"Do you think your mother and brothers and I are going to bow to you?" he asked. "Don't be foolish!"

Soon after this his brothers took their father's flocks to Shechem to find pastures for them there. Shechem was a long way off. It took several days to walk there with the sheep.

Not long afterwards Jacob said to Joseph, "Go and find your brothers and see how they are getting along and how the sheep are." So Joseph went to find them.

But his brothers weren't at Shechem. He was wandering around in the fields looking for them when he met a man who told him, "Your brothers are at Dothan. I heard them say that they were going there." So Joseph went on to Dothan.

When his brothers saw him coming, they began talking to each other about killing him.

"Here comes that dreamer," they said. "Come on, let's kill him and throw him into a well, and we'll say some wild animal has eaten him. Then we'll see what happens to his dreams!"

When Joseph's brother Reuben heard them talking like that, he didn't like it at all. He wanted to save Joseph, so he persuaded his brothers to put Joseph into the well without hurting him. Reuben planned to come back after the others were gone and take Joseph out and get him home to his father again.

Joseph came, and they grabbed him and took away his beautiful coat and put him into a well that did not have any water in it.

Then they sat down to eat their lunches. Just then they saw some men coming along on camels: these men were taking things to the country of Egypt to sell. When Joseph's brother Judah saw them, he said, "Let's sell Joseph to them! We'll get rid of him and get some money, too."

The other brothers thought this was a good idea, so they pulled Joseph out of the well and sold him for twenty pieces of silver. The merchants put him on a camel and took him far away to the land of Egypt.

The brothers killed a young goat and dipped Joseph's coat in the blood. They brought the coat to their father and told him they had found it on the ground.

"Is it Joseph's coat?" they asked.

Jacob gives his son Joseph a beautiful coat

Jacob knew it was and began to cry. "Yes," he said, "it is Joseph's coat; a wild animal must have eaten him. Joseph is dead."

Then Jacob tore his clothing and dressed himself in sackcloth. Sackcloth is a dark, scratchy kind of cloth that people used to wear to show their sadness. Jacob said that he would mourn

for his boy all the rest of his life.

QUESTIONS
Why were Joseph's brothers angry with him?
What did they do?
What else did they do that was wrong?

IO

Joseph in Jail

The men who had bought Joseph took him to Egypt and sold him to a man named Potiphar, who was an Egyptian army officer. Joseph became his slave and lived in his house.

The Lord helped Joseph to work hard. His master was pleased with him and put him in charge of all his other servants. God blessed Potiphar because Joseph was in his home.

But after awhile Potiphar's wife wanted Joseph to do something very wrong. Joseph said no, and that made her angry. She decided to get even with him, so she told her husband a lie. She said that Joseph had tried to hurt her. Her husband believed her and put Joseph in jail.

But the Lord was kind to Joseph and made the man in charge of the prison feel friendly to him. He put him in charge of all the other prisoners. Joseph took the full responsibility of taking care of them. And the Lord

helped Joseph do everything just the way it should be done.

One day Pharaoh, the king of Egypt, became angry with two of his officers; one of them was his baker, and the other was the man who brought him wine whenever he wanted a drink. Pharaoh put them both in the jail where Joseph was.

One night both of these men had dreams. When Joseph came in to see them the next morning, they looked very sad.

"What's the matter?" he asked. "Why so sad this morning?"

"We had strange dreams last night," they told him, "and there is no one to tell us what the dreams mean."

"Tell me your dreams," Joseph said, "and I'll ask God what they mean."

So they did, and Joseph was able to tell them what their dreams meant.

He said they meant that the two men would get out of jail.

"When you get out, don't forget about me!" Joseph said. "Ask the king to let me out, too."

Then Joseph told him how he had been sold by his brothers and brought to Egypt. He said he had done nothing wrong and shouldn't be in jail.

I'm sorry to say that the men promptly forgot all about Joseph and didn't bother to tell Pharaoh about him or try to get him out of jail.

Two years later King Pharaoh had a dream. He was standing beside the Nile River in Egypt and saw seven cows coming up out of the water. They were fat and healthy, and they went into a meadow to eat grass. Then seven more cows came up out of the river. These cows were thin and scrawny, and they ate the fat and healthy cows! Just then King Pharaoh woke up.

Soon he went back to sleep and had another dream. This time he thought he saw seven ears of corn growing on one stalk. They were plump ears, well filled with grain. But afterwards seven other ears of corn grew on the stalk. These were thin and withered, and they ate up the seven good ears! Then Pharaoh woke up and realized it was all a dream.

The dreams bothered him so much that he sent for all the wise men of Egypt and told them his dreams, but they couldn't tell the king what his dreams meant.

Then the man in charge of the king's wine remembered the young man in jail who had told him and the chief baker what their dreams meant. He remembered that the dreams came true just as Joseph had said.

So the king sent for Joseph. He quickly shaved and put on other clothes and was brought to Pharaoh.

Pharaoh said to Joseph, "I had a dream last night, and no one can tell me what it means; but I'm told that you can."

Joseph said he could not do it, but that God would. Then Pharaoh told Joseph his dreams: the one about the seven thin cows who ate the seven fat ones and still looked so thin and starved afterwards; and the dream about the shriveled-up ears of corn eating the fat ears of corn.

Joseph told him that both dreams meant the same thing: God was telling Pharaoh what was going to happen in the future. The seven fat cows and the seven good ears of corn meant seven years of wonderful crops, when everyone's gardens would grow; and the seven thin cows and the seven withered ears of corn meant seven years when nothing would grow. First there would be seven good years in Egypt. The corn would grow tall, and there would be plenty to eat. But afterwards there would be seven years of poor crops when people would be hungry, for nothing would grow in their gardens.

Joseph told Pharaoh to put someone in charge of making the people of Egypt save up corn during the seven good years. Then during the hungry years, the people would have enough food. The king thought this was a good idea and he put Joseph in charge!

QUESTIONS

Why was Joseph put in prison?

How did Joseph know what all the dreams meant?

What did Pharaoh dream?

Why do you think he put Joseph in charge of the people?

II

Joseph Meets His Brothers

So Pharaoh didn't send Joseph back to jail any more, but made a great man of him instead. The king took off his own ring and put it on Joseph's finger and dressed him in beautiful clothing and put a gold chain around his neck.

He gave him a chariot to ride in, with soldiers running along ahead of him shouting, "Bow down." And all the people bowed low before him wherever he went. He was in charge of all the land of Egypt and was almost as great as the king. Everyone had to do whatever Joseph told him to do.

During the first seven years, when all the farms had such good crops, he went to all the farmers and made them give some of their corn to Pharaoh. Joseph took this grain and stored it in the nearby cities, keeping it safe until the seven years of famine came. Soon he had so much grain stored away that he stopped counting it.

Then the seven years of good crops ended, and the seven years of poor crops began. Soon everyone began to be hungry because there was so little to eat. When all their food was gone,

the people came to Pharaoh to ask for something to eat.

"Joseph is in charge," Pharaoh said, "Go to him and he will tell you what to do."

Then Joseph opened up the buildings where the grain was kept and sold it to the people.

Joseph's brothers were still living in the land of Canaan when the famine came. Soon their grain was gone, and they needed food for their father and for their families. They looked at each other blankly, not knowing what to do.

Then their father said to them, "Don't just stand around looking at each other! I hear there is grain in Egypt; go and buy some for us, so we won't starve to death."

So Joseph's ten brothers got on their donkeys and rode for many days until they came to Egypt. Joseph's youngest brother, Benjamin, stayed with his father in Canaan, for his father was afraid to let him go. He was afraid something might happen to him just as it had to Joseph.

Since Joseph was the governor of Egypt, he was in charge of selling the

grain to the people. But his brothers
didn't recognize him in his Egyptian
robes. They came and bowed low before him, never imagining he was
their brother! But Joseph knew them
right away.

Do you remember Joseph's dream
that had made his brothers so angry?
He had dreamed that his brothers'
sheaves of grain bowed to his sheaf,
and that the sun and moon and eleven
stars had bowed to him. And now it
had come true—here were his brothers
bowing to him now!

Imagine Joseph's surprise and joy
to see his brothers again, even though
they had been so cruel to him. But
he pretended he didn't know them at
all. He spoke roughly to them and
asked them, "Where are you from?"

"From the land of Canaan," they
said. "We have come to buy food."

Then Joseph said, "No, you are
spies and have come here to see what
trouble we are in, so that you can
bring an army and attack us."

Then he put them in jail for three
days.

On the third day he talked with
them again. This time he said that
only one of them must stay, and all
the others could go home to take food
to their families. One must stay so
that Joseph would be sure the others
would come back again and bring
their youngest brother with them.

Then he took Simeon and tied him
up while all the others watched, for
Simeon was the one he chose to stay
in Egypt while the others went home
after Benjamin.

Then Joseph told his servants to
fill his brothers' sacks with grain and
to put into the tops of their sacks the
money they had paid for the grain;

The Egyptians save their corn during the seven good years

but he didn't tell his brothers that the money was there.

Finally their donkeys were loaded, and all except Simeon started back home to Canaan. That night when they stopped to eat, they opened a sack to get some food. There was the money right at the top of the sack! They were frightened, for they didn't know how it got there.

QUESTIONS

Why did Joseph's brothers come to Egypt?

Did Joseph and his brothers recognize each other?

Why did Joseph keep Simeon in prison?

Why did Reuben think they were having so much trouble?

Why do you think Joseph put the money in the sacks?

12

Joseph's Favorite Brother

After many hard days of travel Joseph's brothers finally returned home and told their father what had happened.

When they went out to unload their donkeys and empty the grain out of their sacks, can you imagine their surprise when each of them found his money at the top of his sack? There it was, lying right on top of the grain! When Jacob saw the money, he was afraid.

The famine became worse and worse. Soon the grain brought from Egypt was almost gone and Jacob said to his sons, "Go back to Egypt again, and buy us a little more food."

But Judah told his father they couldn't go unless Benjamin was with

them; for the governor had told them, "You must not return without your brother."

"But why did you tell him you had another brother?" Jacob cried out.

"The man asked us," they replied. "He said, 'Is your father still living? Have you another brother?' How could we know he would say, 'You must bring your brother here?'"

Then Judah told his father he would take care of Benjamin.

"I'll see that nothing happens to him," Judah said, "and if I don't bring him safely back again, then I will bear the blame forever. If we had not stayed home so long, we could have gone to Egypt and been back by now."

Finally their father agreed. He told his sons to take a present to the governor.

"Take some honey, spices and myrrh, and nuts and almonds. Take extra money with you, along with the money that came back in your sacks before; perhaps it was a mistake. And take your brother, and go."

Then Jacob prayed for his sons and begged God to make the governor kind to them; for if his children were taken away from him, he would die with sorrow.

The brothers took the presents, the money, and their brother Benjamin and went back to Egypt. Soon Joseph saw them standing before him again.

When Joseph saw Benjamin with them, he said to his servants, "Take these men home to my house and get dinner ready for them, for they are going to eat with me."

Joseph's brothers were frightened when they saw where the servant was taking them. They thought Joseph was going to keep them as his slaves and never let them go home again. They thought it was because of the money they found in their sacks.

They went to Joseph's servant and told him all that had happened: that when they were going home to Canaan, they had opened their sacks and found their money there. But they hadn't stolen it, and now they had brought it back again.

Joseph's servant told them not to worry, there was nothing to fear. He brought their brother Simeon to them, the one who had been left as a prisoner while they went home for Benjamin.

The servant gave them water to wash their feet and hay for their donkeys. Then they got out the present their father had sent to the governor, to give it to him when he came home at noon, for now they knew they were to eat there.

When Joseph arrived, they brought his present to him and bowed low before him.

He spoke kindly to them and said, "Is your father well, the old man you told me about? Is he still living?"

They answered, "Yes, he is in good health, he is still alive." And they bowed to him again.

Then Joseph saw his brother Benjamin and said, "Is this your youngest brother you told me about? May God be good to you, my son."

Then Joseph hurried away to find a place where he could be alone. He went into his bedroom and started crying because he was so happy at seeing his little brother again. But then he washed his face, and when he came out again he kept back the tears so that his brothers didn't know what he had been doing!

Joseph seated the oldest brother at the head of the table, with the next oldest next to him, and so on down the line according to their ages. Who could have told him their ages, they wondered! But you and I know that no one had to tell him, for he knew it all the time!

QUESTIONS
Why didn't Jacob want Benjamin to go to Egypt?
Why did he send presents?
How did Joseph welcome his brothers?
Why do you think they were surprised when they sat down to eat?

13
A Big Surprise

Joseph told one of his servants to fill the men's sacks with grain and to put back their money in the top of the sacks, just as he had before.

"And," Joseph said, "put my silver cup in the sack of the youngest boy, Benjamin." So that is what the servant did.

In the morning, as soon as it was light, the men got on their donkeys and started happily back to Canaan.

But they were hardly out of the city when Joseph told his servant to chase after them and stop them and ask them why they had stolen his silver cup? So the servant hurried and caught up with them.

They were very much surprised and wondered what the servant was talking about when he asked them about the cup.

"God forbid that we should do such a thing as to steal the governor's cup," they said.

They reminded the servant that they had proved their honesty by bringing back the money they found in their sacks before, and they certainly wouldn't steal a silver cup.

"If any of us stole it, we ourselves will kill him," they said, "and all the rest of us will go back and be slaves."

The servant said that only the one who had stolen the cup would be a slave; the rest of them could go on home.

Then they all took down their sacks from the backs of their donkeys and opened them so the servant could look. He began with the sack of the oldest, but the cup wasn't there. He went on down the line, but none of them had the cup. Then he came to Benjamin. And there was the cup, right at the top of Benjamin's sack.

Now the poor brothers didn't know what to do. They tore their clothes in sorrow and finally loaded up their donkeys and went back to the city with Benjamin and the servant.

When they saw Joseph they all fell to the ground before him. Joseph pretended that he thought Benjamin had really stolen his cup and said they should have known that he would find out about it. Judah stood up and spoke to Joseph for all of them.

"Oh, what shall we say to my lord?" he asked. "God has found out our wickedness; we are all your slaves."

A big surprise for Joseph's brothers

But Joseph said that only the one who had stolen the cup would be his slave; the rest of them could go on home to their father.

Judah pleaded with Joseph. He reminded him about the first time they had come to Egypt for food, and how Joseph had asked them whether they had a father and a brother at home. And they had told him yes, their father was an old man now, and their brother was still very young. They had told him that their father dearly loved his youngest son, for he was all he had left from his wife Rachel, who was dead.

But Joseph had said that they must bring their younger brother to Egypt with them the next time they came. They said then that the boy could not leave his father, for if he did, his father would die. But Joseph had told

them that if they didn't bring their brother, they could never come back.

Judah explained to Joseph that when they went home, they had told their father what he had said. And when their father wanted them to go back to Egypt to buy more food, they had told him, "We can't, unless Benjamin goes with us, for the man told us not to come back without him." Then their father told them that if they took Benjamin, and anything happened to him, he would die of sorrow. So now, Judah said, if they went home without Benjamin, their father would die of shock and sorrow. Then Judah begged Joseph to let him stay and be a slave instead of Benjamin, and to let Benjamin go home to his father.

Joseph couldn't stand it any longer. He ordered all of his servants to leave

the room, and Joseph was left alone with his brothers. Then he began to cry. His brothers watched in surprise.

Finally, when he could speak, he told them, "I am Joseph! Oh, tell me more about my father!"

His brothers were too surprised and frightened to say anything. Then Joseph called them over to him.

"I am your brother Joseph!" he said again.

Then at last they realized what he was saying—and what excitement there was as they all hugged and kissed each other!

Joseph told them to stop being sad for what they had done to him, because God had turned it all into good. Joseph loved his brothers and didn't want them to be unhappy and afraid, and that is why he told them this.

He explained to them that the famine would last another five years, for God had said that there would be no crops for all that time.

"Hurry back to my father," he told them, "and tell him that his son Joseph says, 'God has made me ruler over all of Egypt. Come down to me, and you will live in the best part of the land. Bring your children, your flocks and your herds, and all that you have, and I will take care of you.' Tell my father how great I am in Egypt, and describe all you have seen. Hurry home and bring my father here."

Then Joseph hugged his brother Benjamin and cried again, for he was so glad to see him. And Benjamin cried too, and so did all the brothers.

When Pharaoh heard that Joseph's brothers had come, he was very glad.

He told Joseph to tell them to return for their father and their wives and children and bring them all to Egypt where there was plenty to eat.

"Take some of my wagons for your wives and little ones to ride in," he said, "Don't bother to bring any of your furniture and other things, for I will give you everything you need."

Then Joseph gave new clothes to each of them—giving Benjamin more than any of the others! And he sent his father twenty donkey-loads of food and other good things. Then at last he let his brothers start home again to get his father and their families.

When they finally arrived home, what joy there was!

"Joseph is alive," they shouted. "He is governor over all the land of Egypt!"

It seemed too wonderful to be true, and Jacob did not believe them at first; but when he saw Pharaoh's wagons that he had sent, he finally realized that his sons were telling the truth.

"It is proof enough," he said at last. "Joseph is alive! I will go and see him now before I die."

So Jacob and his children and their families all left their homes in Canaan and went to Egypt to live with Joseph.

QUESTIONS

What did Joseph put in his brothers' sacks?

Why do you think Joseph did not insist that Benjamin stay with him?

Did Joseph forgive his brothers for what they had done to him? Why?

Why did Jacob move to Egypt?

What do you think he felt like when he saw Joseph again?

How did Pharaoh show his friendship for Joseph and his family?

14
The Princess Finds a Baby

After hundreds of years Jacob's children and grandchildren and their children became a great nation in Egypt. There were so many of them that it took many days to count them all.

Then a new king began to rule over Egypt who didn't care anything about Joseph and all he had done to save Egypt. When the new king saw how many of Jacob's descendants there were, he was afraid of them. He thought that some day when his enemies came to fight against him, Jacob's huge family would turn against him and help his enemies, then run away and go back to their own country. He didn't want that to happen; he wanted them always to stay in Egypt as slaves to do his work.

So this wicked king persuaded the Egyptians to treat Jacob's family (now known as the Israelis, or people of Israel) very cruelly. They made slaves of them, making them build houses for the Egyptians and work in their fields. But the more cruelly the Israelis were treated, the more of them there were. God had promised Abraham and Isaac and Jacob that their children would become a great nation, and

now God was doing as He had promised.

Pharaoh told the women who took care of the babies to kill all the Israeli boys as soon as they were born. The girls could live, he said, because they would never be able to fight against him.

But these women feared God and did not obey the king. They let the little boys live, too, and God blessed these women for doing this. Then Pharaoh told all his people that whenever they saw a baby boy among the Israelis, they must throw him into the river so he would drown or be eaten by the crocodiles. What a cruel king he was! But God protected his people from this evil king.

Now I'm going to tell you about what happened to one of the little Israeli babies, whose name was Moses. Moses became one of the greatest men in all the world when he grew up.

His mother and father loved him very much, and they were afraid that the Egyptian king's men would come and take their baby away and kill him. So the baby's mother hid him at home for three months after he was born. Then she made a little basket from the stems of long weeds that grew by the river and smeared the outside of it with tar to keep the water out. It was a little boat that would float safely on the water.

She put her baby in the little boat and floated it out among the bushes at the edge of the river. She told her daughter, whose name was Miriam, to hide there and watch to see what would happen to the baby and to try to help him in any way she could.

Soon a princess came along. She was one of the daughters of Pharaoh and had come to bathe in the river. She and her maids were walking along the river's edge when she saw the little boat in the bushes. She sent one of her maids to get it and bring it to her so that she could open it and see what was inside. And when she opened it, there was a little baby! She felt sorry for him and decided to adopt him as her own son.

"This must be one of the Hebrew children," she exclaimed. Miriam, the baby's sister, had been watching; and now she went over to the king's daughter and asked, "May I go and get one of the Hebrew women to take care of the baby for you?" The princess said yes, so Miriam ran home to get her mother! When her mother came, the princess said to her, "Take care of this baby for me, and I will pay you well!"

So the baby's mother took him home again!

QUESTIONS
Why was the new king cruel to the Israelis?
How did Moses' mother save her baby?
Who found the baby?

15
Moses Runs Away

When the little baby was older, the princess sent for him to come and live in her palace and be her son. She called him Moses, an Egyptian word that means "taken out," because she had taken him out of the water. He lived with her for many years and was a prince.

One day when Moses was grown up, he went home to visit his real father and mother and the other people of Israel to see how they were getting along. While he was with them, he saw an Egyptian hitting an Israeli. Of course this made Moses very angry, for the Israeli was one of his relatives. Moses looked to see if anyone was watching, then killed the Egyptian and hid his body in the sand.

The next day as he was walking around he saw two Israelis quarrelling. He scolded the man who was in the wrong and asked him why he had hit the other man. This made the man who had done wrong very angry.

"You can't tell *me* what to do," he shouted. "Are you going to kill me as you killed that Egyptian yesterday?"

Then Moses realized that someone had seen him kill the Egyptian and that everyone knew about it.

When Pharaoh heard what Moses had done, he wanted to arrest Moses and have him executed for murder; but Moses ran far away to the land of Midian, where Pharaoh couldn't find him. He sat down beside a well trying to think what to do next. Soon some girls came to get some water. There were seven of them, all sisters. They wanted to water their father's flock, but some shepherds who were standing beside the well told them to go away.

Moses told the shepherds to be quiet, and he helped the girls water their flocks. When the girls got home, their father asked why they had come back so quickly. They told him that an Egyptian had saved them from the shepherds and helped them get the water.

"Where is the man?" their father asked. "Why didn't you bring him home with you?" He told them to go back and find him and invite him home for dinner. So Moses went home with them. They all wanted him to stay and help them. He liked it so well that he married one of the girls and lived there many years, caring for their father's sheep.

QUESTIONS
Why did Moses kill the Egyptian?
Why did he run away?
How did he find somewhere to live?

16

God Asks Moses to Help Him

All the time Moses was living in the land of Midian, the Egyptians were being very cruel to the people of Israel. Finally the people of Israel cried to the Lord because of their sufferings, and the Lord heard them and looked down from heaven and pitied them. He decided to send Moses to help them.

One day while Moses was taking care of his sheep out in the country near Mount Horeb, suddenly he saw fire flaming up out of a bush. Moses ran over to see what was happening and saw a strange thing: the bush was on fire but didn't burn up! Just then God called to him from the bush, "Moses! Moses!"

We can hardly imagine how surprised and frightened Moses was, but he said, "Yes, Lord, I am listening." God told him not to come any closer and to take off his sandals because the place where he stood was holy

ground, for God was there.

God said, "I am the God of your fathers—the God of Abraham, Isaac, and Jacob." Moses hid his face, for he was afraid to look upon God.

Then God told him that He had seen the sorrows of the people of Israel, and had heard their cries, and had come down from heaven to set them free from the Egyptians.

There was a new king in Egypt by this time, not the one who had chased Moses out of the country. This new king was called Pharaoh just like all the other kings of Egypt. The Lord told Moses to go to Pharaoh and to tell him to stop hurting the people of Israel and to let them leave Egypt and go back to Canaan. The Lord told Moses he was to lead them out of Egypt and to bring them to that very mountain where He was talking with Moses.

But Moses was afraid to go; he was

Moses and the strange burning bush

afraid that Pharaoh would hurt him or kill him if he said to stop hurting the people of Israel.

But God told him, "I will be with you and help you."

God told Moses to tell the people of Israel that God wanted them to leave Egypt and to follow Moses to a good land where there would be plenty to eat and where everyone would be happy and free.

Moses said he was sure that no one would listen to him or believe that the Lord had really sent him. He had a shepherd's rod in his hand, which the Lord told him to throw on the ground. Moses did, and God made it change into a snake! Moses was afraid of it and ran away.

Then the Lord said, "Grab it by the tail." Moses did, and it was changed back into a shepherd's rod again!

Then the Lord said to Moses, "Put your hand into your coat." When he took it out, his hand had turned white! It was covered with a dreadful disease called leprosy that made it white.

"Put your hand back into your coat again," God said. When Moses took it out this time, it was well again!

God gave Moses power to do these two wonderful miracles so that when the people of Israel saw him do them they would believe that God had sent him. But if they still would not believe him, even after he had done these two miracles, then Moses must take some water out of the Nile River and pour it on the ground, and the water would change to blood!

Moses still didn't want to go, and he began to make one excuse after another. He could not speak well in front of people, he said.

But the Lord told him again to go to Pharaoh, and Moses begged the Lord to send someone else. Then the Lord became angry with Moses for refusing.

Moses had a brother whose name was Aaron. God finally said that Aaron could go with Moses and make the speeches to Pharaoh and the people of Israel. God would tell Moses what to say, Moses would tell Aaron what to say, and Aaron would tell the people and the king what God wanted them to know.

When the Lord had finished talking with him from the burning bush, Moses went back home and received permission from his father-in-law, whose name was Jethro, to return to Egypt to visit his people.

QUESTIONS

What was strange about the bush Moses saw?

What did God tell Moses to do?

What were the two miracles Moses could do?

Why did God become angry with Moses?

17
Pharaoh Won't Listen

The Lord told Moses' brother, Aaron, to go and meet Moses at Mount Horeb. When he got there, Moses told him all about everything that had happened and what God had said for him to do.

Moses and Aaron went together to Egypt and talked with the Israeli leaders, and showed them the two miracles. He threw down his shepherd's rod and it became a snake; then he put his hand into his coat, and it became white with leprosy. When the leaders saw these two miracles, they believed that God had sent Moses and Aaron, and that Moses was to lead them out of Egypt.

Then Moses and Aaron went to Pharaoh and told him, "The Lord God of Israel says, 'Let my people leave Egypt and worship Me in the desert.'"

"Huh!" Pharaoh scoffed. "Who is the Lord, and why should I obey him? I've never heard of that god, and I certainly won't let these Israeli people out of my sight."

Moses and Aaron begged Pharaoh to let the people go. They said that God would punish Pharaoh if he

didn't obey. But Pharaoh was angry. He asked Moses and Aaron what right they had to get the people all excited about going on a trip and keeping them from their work. "Stop this foolishness right now," he shouted. "Get out of here, and get to work!"

One of the jobs of the Israeli slaves was to dig clay and make bricks by drying the clay in the sun. The clay was mixed with pieces of straw to make the bricks tougher and stronger. This straw was given to them by Pharaoh.

But now Pharaoh was so angry that he said from now on they must get their own straw, but still make just as many bricks as before. Pharaoh said they were lazy, and that was why they wanted time to go and worship their God.

So the people of Israel went out into the fields and gathered straw. But though they worked very hard, they could not make as many bricks as when the straw was brought to them. Some of the people were brutally beaten because of this.

The leaders of the people of Israel told Pharaoh that he wasn't being fair. How could he expect them to make as many bricks now that he was not giving them the straw?

He replied, "You're lazy! You're lazy! That's why you say, 'Let us go and sacrifice to the Lord.'" And he told them to get to work, for no straw would be given to them anymore.

Then the Israelis saw that they were in real trouble, and some of them went to Moses and Aaron and accused them of making things worse for them instead of better.

Moses complained to the Lord about it and asked why He had sent him. He had only made things worse for the people, and now the Egyptians were more cruel than before.

"Just wait," the Lord told Moses, "and you'll see what I am going to do. Tell My people that I will rescue them from their slavery, and they will be My special people. I will lead them into the land I promised long ago to Abraham, Isaac, and Jacob."

Moses told the Israelis what God

Pharaoh makes the Israelis work even harder

said, but they wouldn't listen to him anymore.

Then the Lord sent Moses and Aaron to talk to Pharaoh again. "When Pharaoh tells you to do a miracle, throw your shepherd's rod on the ground," the Lord said, "and it will change into a snake, just as it did before."

So Moses and Aaron went to Pharaoh. Aaron threw down his rod, and sure enough, it changed into a snake. Then Pharaoh called for his magicians. They brought some shepherd's rods and threw them down, and their rods changed into snakes too. The Lord let the magicians do just as Aaron had done!

But Aaron's snake swallowed up all the other snakes! Yet even so Pharaoh wouldn't let the people go.

QUESTIONS

Why didn't Pharaoh listen to Moses?

How did Pharaoh punish the people of Israel?

Who was Aaron?

18

The Terrible Troubles Begin

The Lord told Moses to go to Pharaoh the next morning when he would be taking a walk beside the river. When Pharaoh came along, Moses must go up to him and say, "The God of the Hebrews has sent me to tell you, 'Let My people go. They must sacrifice to Me in the desert.' "

So the next morning Moses went to the river. Sure enough, Pharaoh was out for a walk, and Moses told Pharaoh what the Lord had said. But Pharaoh refused to let the people go.

The Lord told Aaron to strike the river with his shepherd's staff, while Pharaoh and his men were watching. When Aaron did this, the water in the river changed to blood! Suddenly all the water in Egypt, in all the streams and ponds, changed to blood too! So the fish died, and the Egyptians had no water to drink.

Then Pharaoh's magicians came; and they, too, turned water into blood, because the Lord let them do it. So Pharaoh went back home to his palace and wouldn't let the people go.

The Egyptians dug holes in the ground near the river to get water fit to drink, for the blood stayed in the river seven days.

The Lord now told Moses to announce to Pharaoh that unless he let the people go, God would send millions of frogs that would cover the entire nation and be in the Egyptians' houses and even jump into their beds.

But Pharaoh said he didn't care, he wouldn't let the people go.

So God told Aaron to point his shepherd's staff over the rivers of Egypt. Suddenly, millions of frogs came up out of the water.

Pharaoh's magicians held out their rods over the rivers, and more frogs came out; for again God allowed them to do the same thing Aaron did.

But now Pharaoh and the people of Egypt were in real trouble. Frogs were everywhere. He called for Moses and Aaron and asked them to pray to God to take the frogs away. "If you do," Pharaoh said, "I'll let the people go to sacrifice in the desert."

"When do you want the frogs to die?" Moses asked.

Pharaoh replied, "Tomorrow."

So the next day Moses prayed to the Lord, and the Lord did as Moses asked. The frogs in the houses and villages and fields all died, and the people gathered them in great heaps. The smell of dead frogs was all over the land. It was terrible!

But when Pharaoh saw that the frogs were dead, he wouldn't let the people go.

Then the Lord commanded Aaron to strike the dust on the ground with his shepherd's staff, and the dust changed into very small insects called lice that covered the people and the cattle.

Pharaoh's magicians tried to make lice, too. But this time they couldn't, because God wouldn't let them. So they told Pharaoh that it was God who had changed the dust to lice. But Pharaoh's heart was wicked. He wouldn't listen, and he wouldn't let the people go.

QUESTIONS
What happened to all the water in Egypt? Why?
What did Pharaoh promise he would do if God took away the frogs?
Did he keep his promise?
Do you think God is pleased when we don't keep our promises?

19
Flies, Boils, and Hail!

The Lord again told Moses to get up early the next morning to meet Pharaoh as he went to bathe in the river. Moses must tell him again to let the people go. If he still refused to let them go, the Lord would send swarms of flies all over Egypt.

Moses did as the Lord commanded, but again Pharaoh said no, he wouldn't let the people go. So the Lord sent the flies and they covered the whole country. The houses of the Egyptians were swarming with them, and the ground was covered with them.

But in the land of Goshen where the Israelis lived, there were no flies at all, because the Lord did not send them there.

Pharaoh was very much upset about the flies, as he had been about the frogs. He called Moses and Aaron and told them, "All right, the people of Israel can sacrifice to their God, but they must stay in Egypt to do it. They mustn't go out into the desert."

Moses told Pharaoh they must leave Egypt and go three days' journey into the desert to sacrifice to the Lord, for that is what God had told them to do.

Then Pharaoh said all right, they could go, but not that far.

"Please," he begged Moses, "pray to your God to get rid of the flies." Moses said he would, but he warned Pharaoh not to lie to him again by not letting the people go. Moses went away and prayed to the Lord, and the Lord took away the swarms of flies from Pharaoh and his people. Suddenly there wasn't one left in all the land! But when Pharaoh saw that the flies were gone, he changed his mind again and wouldn't let the people go.

Next the Lord commanded Moses to tell Pharaoh that a great sickness would destroy the cows and sheep of Egypt, but the cows and sheep of the Israelis would not be hurt at all.

But Pharaoh still said no, the people could not go.

So the Lord sent the sickness. The Egyptian cows and horses and donkeys and camels and sheep began to die. Pharaoh sent to see if any of the Israelis' cattle were dead, but not one of them was even sick! When Pharaoh found that the animals belonging to the people of Israel were all right, his heart grew even harder and more wicked than before, and he would not let the people go!

Then the Lord told Moses and Aaron to stand where Pharaoh could see them and to toss handfuls of ashes into the air. Those ashes, the Lord said, would cause terrible sores to break out all over the bodies of the Egyptians and their animals. So Moses stood before Pharaoh and tossed the ashes into the air; and the sores broke out on the Egyptians and on their animals throughout all Egypt, except where the Israelis lived. This time the magicians didn't even try to do the same thing, for the terrible boils were on them, too.

But Pharaoh's heart was still wicked, and he wouldn't let the people go!

Then the Lord told Moses to get up early the next morning and tell Pharaoh that God would send a great hailstorm—a storm such as there had never been before. Moses told Pharaoh to quickly get all his cattle in from the fields, for everything out in the storm would die. Some of the Egyptians feared the Lord, and when they heard what was going to happen, they brought in their slaves and cattle from the fields and put them in barns where the hail couldn't hurt them. But most of the Egyptians didn't believe what Moses said and left their animals out in the fields anyway.

Then the Lord told Moses to point his hand toward heaven, and suddenly a terrible hailstorm began, and lightning ran along the ground. Never before had there been such a storm in Egypt. The hail crashed down onto the fields, killing men and animals alike. It broke the bushes and trees, and all the grain was broken and spoiled, except for what hadn't yet grown up above the ground.

But in the land of Goshen, where the people of Israel lived, no hail fell at all!

Then Pharaoh sent for Moses and Aaron and said, "I have sinned; the Lord is good, and I and my people are wicked. Beg the Lord to stop the terrible thunder and hail, and I will let you go right away."

Moses said that as soon as he was out of the city he would ask the Lord to stop the thunder and hail. But he knew that Pharaoh still wouldn't obey

Flies everywhere

the Lord. Moses went out into the terrible storm, but God kept the hail and fire from harming him. When he was out of the city he prayed, and the thunder and hail stopped.

And when Pharaoh saw that it had stopped, he changed his mind and wouldn't let the people go!

Moses and Aaron went to Pharaoh again to tell him that if he wouldn't obey the Lord, tomorrow the Lord would send locusts to destroy everything that was left. Locusts are like grasshoppers, but they eat gardens and crops.

Once again Pharaoh refused to let the people of Israel worship God, and so great clouds of locusts came. Again Pharaoh promised, so God took the locusts away by sending a strong wind to blow them into the Red Sea. But Pharaoh changed his mind and wouldn't let the people go.

Then the Lord commanded Moses

to hold up his hand toward heaven, and it became dark all over the land. The Egyptians couldn't see one another for three days, and couldn't leave their homes.

But in the houses of the Israelis it was as light as usual.

Then Pharaoh called for Moses, and said, "All right, go and worship the Lord! Take your children with you, but not your flocks and herds." But Moses told him no, they wouldn't go without their animals. That made Pharaoh angry. He told Moses again to get out of his sight and never come back again. If he did, Pharaoh said, he would kill him.

QUESTIONS
What three plagues did God send?
Why weren't the Israelis hurt by them?
Did Pharaoh keep his promise?
What did the locusts do?
Did Pharaoh give in?
What did Pharaoh tell Moses to do?

20
The Worst Plague of All

Moses became angry and told Pharaoh that God was going to send one last terrible punishment. The Lord Himself was coming to Egypt and in the middle of some night soon, He would cause the oldest son in every Egyptian home to die. Even

Pharaoh's oldest son would die. There would be a great cry of grief all through the land, such crying as there had never been before and would never be again. But not one of the Israeli children would be hurt in any way; then Pharaoh would know that

The Israelis mark the doors of their houses

he and his people were the ones the Lord was punishing, and not the Israelis. Moses told Pharaoh that after this punishment the Egyptians would come and beg Moses to take his people and leave the country.

Moses stalked out in great anger, leaving Pharaoh sitting there.

Then the Lord instructed the Israelis to be ready to leave Egypt in four days. He said to ask the Egyptians for jewels and silver earrings and gold necklaces to take with them. And the Lord caused the Egyptians to want to give their jewels to the people of Israel.

The Lord said for each family in Israel to get a lamb and to kill it on the fourth evening. Then they must take the blood of the lamb outside and sprinkle it on each side of the door and up above the door, making three marks of blood on the outside of every Israeli home. They must stay in their houses and not come out again until morning, for that night the angel of the Lord would come and kill the oldest child in every home where the blood was not on the door.

On that fourth evening they must roast the lamb, God said, and everyone in the house must eat some of it. They must be dressed to travel as they ate it, all ready to go, with their shoes on and their walking sticks in their hands. And they were to hurry as they ate, for when the Lord went through the land on that night and caused the oldest sons to die, at last Pharaoh would really let them go.

God promised that He would pass over the houses where the blood was on the door and not harm anyone inside. The supper of lamb they ate that night was called the Lord's "Pass-

over," because the Lord passed over the houses where He saw the blood on the door.

At last the terrible night came. In the middle of the night the Lord passed through the land. Wherever He saw the marks of blood, He passed over that house and no one there was harmed. But there were no marks of blood on the houses of the Egyptians, and the Lord sent his destroying angel into every one of those homes and caused the oldest son to die. Even Pharaoh's oldest son died that night.

The king got up in the night with all his people, and there was a great cry of sorrow and despair through all the land, for in every home the oldest son was dead.

Pharaoh called for Moses and Aaron and told them to leave Egypt at once and to take all the people of Israel with them. "Take all your flocks and herds," he begged, "and leave to-night." All the Egyptians begged them to go quickly, for they were afraid the Lord would kill them all, not just their oldest sons.

So the people of Israel left Egypt that night, carrying their clothes on their shoulders. And the Egyptians gave them jewels of silver and gold, and clothes too; so they went away with great riches. And many of the Egyptians went with them.

The lamb that was killed in every Israeli home that night was in some ways like our Saviour. The lamb died for the people, and its blood saved them. That is what happened again many years later, when Christ the Saviour came as the Lamb of God to die for each of us.

And just as God passed over those who had the marks of the lamb's blood on their houses, and did not punish them, so it will be when Christ comes back again. He will not punish those who have the marks of the Saviour's blood in their hearts—those whose hearts have been cleansed from sin by His blood.

QUESTIONS
What was the worst plague?
What did the Israelis do to keep away the Angel of Death?
Why was their meal called the "Passover"?

21

The Fire Cloud

Finally the people of Israel had escaped from Egypt. At last they were free. What a wonderful feeling it must have been—they were no longer Pharaoh's slaves.

The Lord led them toward the Red Sea to a place called Etham, on the edge of the desert. There they set up their tents and made camp.

As they travelled along, the Lord was very kind to them; He went before them in a cloud to show them the way. The cloud was shaped like a pillar reaching up toward heaven. They could see it all the time. As they walked along, it moved on ahead of them so that they could follow it and know where God wanted them to go. In the daylight it looked like a cloud, but at night it became a pillar of fire. It gave them light at night, so they could travel whenever the Lord wanted them to, day or night.

The Israelis now found themselves in a great desert between Egypt and the Promised Land, Canaan, where God was leading them. Soon their water was gone and they were thirsty. They finally arrived at a place called Marah and found water there, but it was too bitter to drink. But instead of asking the Lord to help them, they blamed Moses.

Moses prayed to the Lord about it, and the Lord showed him a certain tree and told him to throw it into the water. He did, and suddenly the water was no longer bitter, and the people could drink it!

They travelled on and came to Elim; there were twelve wells there and seventy palm trees. Going on farther they came to the desert of Sihn. But now a rebellion broke out; the people began to riot against Moses and Aaron because they were hungry. They said they had had plenty of food in Egypt and they wished God had

killed them there instead of bringing
them out into the desert to die of
starvation.

The Lord heard their complaints
and told Moses He would send meat
for them that evening, and as much

bread as they wanted in the morning.
Then they would know that the Lord
was taking care of them.

The Lord did as He promised; for
that evening about the time the sun

was going down, huge flocks of birds called quail came flying just above the ground. The people killed them with clubs and ate them for supper.

The next morning after the dew was gone, small, white, round things were all over the ground. No one knew what it was, so they called it "manna," which in their language means, "What is it?"

"This is the bread the Lord promised you," Moses told them.

The Lord told the people to go out each day except Saturday and gather as much as they wanted. He told them not to take more than they needed for one day, since there would be a fresh supply each morning. The Lord wanted them to trust Him one day at a time for their daily bread. Some of the people didn't obey, and gathered enough for two days instead of one. The next morning the extra manna was spoiled, with worms crawling around in it. They had to throw it away and get fresh manna off the ground.

Each morning when the sun warmed the ground the manna melted away and disappeared. But early the next morning there was always more waiting for them.

The only exception was on the seventh day of each week. That was the Sabbath day when God told them not to work. On that day there was no manna on the ground. The day before the Sabbath they gathered twice as much as other days, and what they saved to eat the next day didn't spoil. Some of the people went out on the Sabbath anyway to try to get some, but there wasn't any. And the Lord was angry, so they didn't do it anymore. After that they rested on the

Sabbath day as the Lord had told them to.

The manna was small and round, and white like coriander seed. It tasted like bread made with honey. Moses told Aaron to get a bottle and fill it with manna. He wanted to keep it forever, so that the children who weren't even born yet would be able to see a sample of the food the Lord fed His people with in the desert. Moses did this, and God kept the manna from spoiling for hundreds of years until they finally lost it.

The Israelis ate manna every day for forty years until they finally came to the land of Canaan.

As they travelled they came to a place called Rephidim, but found no water there. So they complained again. "Get us water," they demanded of Moses.

"Why blame me?" Moses asked.

"Because you brought us here," they retorted.

Then Moses cried out to the Lord and said, "What shall I do? For they are almost ready to stone me."

By this time they were close to Mount Horeb where Moses had seen the fire burning in the bush. The Lord told him to lead the people to a certain rock on Mount Horeb and to strike the rock with his walking stick. Moses did as the Lord said, and water poured out giving everyone enough to drink!

QUESTIONS

How did God guide the people through the wilderness?

What happened when the people collected more manna than they needed for one day?

Why didn't God want the people to collect any manna on the Sabbath?

Moses and the Israelis follow God's cloud

God sends food from heaven

22
God's Commandments

Then God gave the people of Israel these Ten Commandments:

1
You Must Not Have Any Other God But Me

This means that we must love God more than anyone or anything else; for anything we love more than God becomes our god instead of Him.

2
You Must Not Make Any Idol, nor Bow Down to One, nor Worship It

Many people in the world make statues, or idols, and believe that they are gods which can help them. But in this commandment God forbids making such statues or bowing down to them or worshipping them. God is the only One who can save men, and we are to worship Him alone. This commandment also means that we are not to worship money or clothes or anything else but God.

3
You Must Not Take the Name of the Lord Your God in Vain

This means that whenever we speak God's name, we must do it reverently, remembering how great and holy a name it is. If we speak it carelessly or thoughtlessly, we offend Him. This commandment teaches us not to swear.

4
Remember the Sabbath Day, to Keep It Holy

In this commandment God instructed His people not to work on the Sabbath. This was because God rested on the seventh day after His six days of work when He created the heavens and the earth.

5
Honor Your Father and Your Mother

Next to obeying God, we should obey our parents. We must not delay doing what they tell us to, and shouldn't even wait to be told. This is God's commandment.

6
You Must Not Kill

We break this commandment by murdering, but we also break it when we are angry with someone and wish he were dead. For then we have the wish for his death in our hearts, and God sees murder in our hearts.

7
You Must Not Commit Adultery

When a man lives with a woman as his wife when he is already married to somebody else, it is adultery. God says we must never do this, and it is a sin when a man and a woman sleep together when they are not married. He commands us to be pure in all our thoughts, words, and actions.

8
You Must Not Steal

You must not take anything for your own that belongs to someone else. If you have ever done this, whether by mistake or on purpose, God commands you to give it back or pay for it.

9
You Must Not Tell Lies

This means that you must never say anything about another person that isn't true. And when you are saying what is true, you must be very careful how you say it. Don't leave out a little or add a little to make it different from the real truth.

10
You Must Not Covet Anything That Is Your Neighbor's

To covet a thing is to wish it were yours. We must not do this. God, who knows best, gives to each of us just what He wants us to have.

When all the people heard the terrible thunder and the blast of the trumpet and saw the lightning and the smoke and heard God's voice, they were terrified. They said to Moses, "You tell us what God wants, and we will do it; but don't let God speak with us, or we will die." Moses told them God hadn't come down to kill them, but to make them afraid to sin against Him.

The people stood a long way off from the mountain while Moses climbed up to the dark cloud where God was. There God talked with him and gave him many more laws for the Israelis to obey.

When the people heard these laws, they promised to obey all of them.

QUESTIONS
See how many of the Ten Commandments you can remember.
What did the people promise?
What does it mean to "covet"? Do we covet things today?

God gives Moses the Ten Commandments

23
Aaron Makes an Idol

When the Lord had finished talking with Moses, He gave him the two tablets of stone on which God had written the Ten Commandments. Moses had been with God on Mount Sinai for forty days and forty nights learning about all the things God wanted made.

Meanwhile the people of Israel were in their camp at the foot of the mountain. They became impatient when Moses stayed so long. They went to Aaron and said, "We don't know what has become of Moses. We want to worship idols, like all the other nations do."

"All right," Aaron said, "bring me your wives' and children's gold earrings." Aaron melted the earrings in a fire and poured out the gold into a big lump, which he then made into the shape of a beautiful gold calf.

The people bowed to the calf and said it was their god who had brought them out of the land of Egypt. Aaron built an altar in front of it and told the people to come back the next day for a big celebration. Early the next morning, they sacrificed burnt offerings to the calf instead of to the Lord. They had a great party, feasting and getting drunk and dancing around the calf.

All this time Moses was still on the mountain. He couldn't see what the people were doing, but God could. "Quick! Go on down," God told him, "for the people have done a very wicked thing. They have made a calf and worshipped it and sacrificed to it and called it their god."

Moses hurried down the mountain with the two tablets of stone in his hand. Joshua, his helper, was with him; and as they came near the camp, they heard the noise of the people shouting.

Joshua said to Moses, "It sounds as if they are getting ready for war."

"No," Moses said, "it isn't the noise of war; they are singing."

When they came nearer Moses looked down and saw the gold calf and the people dancing before it. He could hardly believe it; in great anger he hurled the two tables of stone down the mountain and they broke in pieces as they smashed against the ground.

QUESTIONS
How long a time was Moses with God on Mount Sinai?
Why was it wrong to sacrifice to the gold calf?
What happened to the two stone tablets?

The people want to worship idols

24
The Idol Is Smashed

When Moses saw the people worshipping the gold calf, he ran all the rest of the way down the mountain and smashed the calf and ground it into powder. Then he threw the powder into the water and made the people drink it.

Moses turned to Aaron and demanded, "Why have you helped the people do this great sin?" Aaron tried to excuse himself. He said the people told him to make the calf or they would hurt him. They brought him their gold, he said, and when he put it into the fire, it just happened to come out in the shape of a calf. What a wicked thing for Aaron to say!

A terrible punishment from the Lord came upon His people because of their sin. Moses stood at the gate of the camp and said for everyone who was on the Lord's side to come and stand there with him. All the men of the tribe of Levi came. He told them to take their swords and to go from one end of the camp to the other killing every man they met. In this way God punished the people for their wickedness. That day the Levites killed about three thousand men.

The next day Moses told the people that although they had sinned so greatly he would pray for them, and perhaps their sin would be forgiven. So he talked with the Lord about it. He confessed that the people had sinned terribly because they had made the idol and worshipped it, but he begged God to forgive them. But God said no, He would punish those who had sinned. He would not go with them to the Promised Land and He would not give them the cloud to lead them any more.

Moses begged God to stay with them, and the Lord finally listened to his prayer and promised that He would.

Then God told Moses to make two stone tablets like the ones he had broken, and He would write the Ten Commandments on them again.

He told Moses to come up alone to the top of the mountain in the morning. No one could be anywhere near the mountain, and no flocks or herds were to graze there.

So Moses chipped out two tablets of rock, just like those he had broken, and went up to the top of Mount

Sinai early in the morning, carrying the tablets. And the Lord came down in the cloud and passed before him. When Moses heard His voice, he bowed quickly to the earth and worshipped. He prayed again that the Lord would forgive the people of Israel and would let them be His people again.

The Lord accepted Moses' prayer and took the people back again as His own. He promised that He would do wonderful things for them and drive out the wicked nations of Canaan to make room for His people to live there instead.

QUESTIONS
Why did Aaron lie to Moses?
How did God punish the people?
Did God answer Moses' prayer?

25
Balaam's Donkey Speaks!

As the Israelis traveled, they came to the plains of Moab, where Balak was the king.

When Balak saw them coming, he was frightened. He thought they wanted to fight with him, and he knew there were too many of them for his soldiers to win against. So he sent a man named Balaam to curse the people of Israel. To curse someone means to ask God to send some great evil upon him. King Balak thought God would hurt the people of Israel if Balaam asked Him to, because Balaam was said to have great power with God.

The king told Balaam he would make him rich and great if he would curse the people of Israel.

Balaam loved money, so although the people of Israel had done him no harm, he was willing to curse them to get the money the king promised to give him. He got up early in the morning, saddled his donkey, and started off with the men whom the king had sent to bring him.

But God was angry with Balaam for agreeing to curse His people. So God sent an angel with a sword to stand in front of Balaam in the road. Balaam couldn't see the angel, but his donkey did and ran into the field by the side of the road to get away. Balaam beat the donkey and told her to behave!

The angel went on further and stood in the road at a place where

Balaam's donkey talks to him

there was a wall on each side. When the donkey came to the place, she pressed up very close to the wall to get by the angel; but in doing this she crushed Balaam's foot against the wall, and he hit her again.

Then the angel went on still further and stood in a narrow place where there was no room at all to get by. The donkey saw the angel standing there with the sword and was so afraid that she fell down under Balaam. This made Balaam very angry, and he beat her as hard as he could.

Then the Lord made the donkey speak like a person! She said, "What have I done to deserve your hitting me these three times?"

Balaam said it was because she had disobeyed him and had turned off the road when he wanted her to go straight ahead. "If I had a sword with me, I'd kill you," Balaam said.

Then the donkey spoke to him again and said, "Haven't you ridden on me ever since I was yours until today? And have I ever done anything like this before?"

"No," Balaam said, "you haven't."

Then the Lord opened Balaam's eyes, and he saw the angel standing there in front of him with a sword, ready to kill him. Balaam was very frightened and threw himself flat on the ground before the angel. Then the angel said to him, "Why have you struck your donkey these three times? I came here to stop you from doing wrong. The donkey saw me and got out of the way. If she hadn't, I would have killed you and saved her alive."

QUESTIONS

Why did Balak send for Balaam?
Why did Balaam's donkey keep stopping?

26

A New Leader

When Moses died, the Lord said to Joshua, "Moses is dead, and you must lead the Israelis across the Jordan River into the land I promised them. Be strong and brave, and be careful to obey all of My laws. Then everything you do will be successful. Don't be afraid, for I will be with you and help you wherever you go."

Then Joshua spoke to the Israeli officers. "Go through the camp," he said, "and announce to all the people that three days from now we will cross the Jordan River into Canaan, the Promised Land!"

Meanwhile, Joshua had already sent two spies across. They came to the city of Jericho and went into the house of a woman named Rahab. Someone told the king of Jericho that two spies had come to the city and were at Rahab's house, so the king sent police officers to Rahab's home and told her to bring out the men who were hiding there.

Instead, Rahab took the two men up to the flat roof of her house and hid them under some stalks of flax spread there to dry. The king's messengers looked all over, but since they couldn't find them, they finally went away.

After they were gone, Rahab talked with the men and said she knew that the Lord had given her country to the Israelis. The people of Canaan had already heard how the God of Israel had dried up a path for them through the Red Sea and how He had helped them in fighting against their enemies. Rahab said that when her people heard these things they were very much afraid of the people of Israel. Then she asked the two men to promise that they would remember her kindness in protecting them, and not let any of her family be killed when Israel captured the city of Jericho.

The men said that if she would keep it a secret about their being there, they would protect her. They told her to hang a red rope from the window of her house to help them recognize it again. When the Israeli army came to destroy the city, no one inside her house would be harmed.

The city of Jericho had a high wall

around it, and Rahab's house was built on the wall. The king had ordered the gates of the city closed to keep the two spies from getting away, so Rahab let the two men down by a rope on the outside of the wall. She warned them to hide in a nearby mountain for three days until the soldiers quit looking for them.

They did this, then crossed the river to tell Joshua all that had happened.

Joshua and all the people got up early the next morning and travelled to the banks of the Jordan River, where they stayed for three days. Then Joshua told them, "Get ready! Tomorrow we will cross the river, and the Lord will do wonders among you. The priests will go first, carrying the Ark. As soon as their feet touch the water, the river will stop flowing, and the priests will walk through on dry ground!"

Everything happened just as Joshua had said. The next morning the priests carried the Ark toward the river, and all the people followed them. When the priests stepped into the water at the river's edge, the water opened up in front of them, and they walked on dry ground into the middle of the river! The priests waited there with the Ark while all the people walked past them to the other side, into the Promised Land of Canaan!

After all the people were across, the priests carrying the Ark followed. As soon as they stepped out of the river onto the shore, the river began flowing again!

The Israelis made their camp at a place called Gilgal. There they found some corn in the fields, which they roasted and ate. It was the first time they had eaten anything but manna for forty years! The next day, the manna stopped coming. For the forty years while they were in the wilderness where no grain grew, the Lord had sent manna to them every morning without fail. But in Canaan there was plenty of food, so the Lord stopped sending the manna.

QUESTIONS

How did Rahab help the spies?
How did the Israelis cross the river Jordan?
Can you remember when something like this happened before?
Why was there no manna in Canaan?

Rahab helps the spies

27
The High Walls Fall Down

Joshua left the camp and went on foot to inspect the city of Jericho with its high walls. Glancing up, he saw a man with a sword in his hand. Joshua strode up to him. "Are you friend or foe?" he demanded.

"I am the general-in-chief of the Lord's army," the man replied. He was telling Joshua that he had come to be their leader and to show them how to win the battles against their enemies. Joshua realized that this Man was the Lord, so he fell to the ground and worshipped Him. It was the same Man who had come to Abraham's tent long before to say that God was going to destroy Sodom. And he was the Man who had wrestled with Jacob when he was returning to Canaan from Laban's house.

The people of Jericho had shut the city gates to stop the Israelis from coming in. But the Lord said He would give Joshua the victory anyway. He even told him how to plan his attack.

All the Israeli soldiers, He said, must march around the city once every day for six days; and the priests must go with them carrying the Ark.

Seven priests were to walk ahead of the Ark, blowing trumpets made of ram's horns.

On the seventh day the Israelis were to march around Jericho, not once, but seven times while the priests blew the trumpets. As they finished the seventh time around, the priests must blow a loud, long blast, and all the army must give a mighty shout. Then the walls of the city would fall down flat, and the Israelis could walk right in!

Joshua told his army that only Rahab and those with her in her house would be saved alive. The Lord had commanded that all the rest of the people of Jericho must die for their sins. All the silver, gold, brass, and iron in the city belonged to the Lord and must be put into the treasury where gifts to the Lord were kept. Joshua told the people not to take any of it for themselves, for the Lord would send a great punishment upon them if they did.

The people did as the Lord commanded. The first day they all marched around the city once, the priests following behind blowing the

The walls of Jericho come tumbling down

trumpets. Then came other priests who carried the Ark.

On the second day they marched around the city again, and so it went for six days.

But on the seventh day they got up early, before it was light, and marched around the city seven times. The last time around, the priests blew a great blast on the trumpets, and Joshua called out to his army, "Shout, for the Lord has given you the city!"

They gave a mighty shout, and at that moment the walls of the city tumbled down before them, and they rushed into Jericho and captured it.

Joshua told the spies who had been at Rahab's house to protect Rahab and everyone with her, just as they had promised her. So they saved Rahab, her father and mother, her brothers, and all who were with her in the house. Afterwards the army of Israel burned the city; but the silver, gold, iron, and bronze were put into the treasury of the Lord.

QUESTIONS
Who was the Man who spoke to Joshua?
What did he tell the Israeli army to do?
What happened?
Why was Rahab saved?

28

Gideon and His Wool

Gideon became the leader of Israel after Joshua died. Soon a great army of Midianites arrived and camped in the valley of Jezreel to fight against Israel. Gideon blew a trumpet and called the men of Israel to go with him and fight them.

Gideon asked God to do a miracle to prove to him that it was really God who had promised to help him when he went to fight against the Midianites. This is the miracle Gideon asked God to do. Gideon said he would leave some wool out on the ground all night. In the morning, if the wool

was wet with dew and the ground all around it was dry, this would be a miracle and he would know that the Lord was going to help him in his fight to free the people of Israel.

So Gideon left the wool on the ground all night. Early the next morning he went out and found it full of water. He wrung the dew out of it with his hands and filled a bowl with the water, but the ground all around was dry! Why wasn't the ground wet too? You see, it was a miracle.

Then Gideon asked the Lord for permission to try it again; but this

Gideon's soldiers drink from the river

time he asked God to make the ground wet with dew and to let the wool stay dry! God agreed, so Gideon left the wool out another night, and in the morning the wool was perfectly dry, but the ground all around was wet!

Gideon knew by these miracles that the Lord would certainly help him when he went out to fight against the Midianites. Gideon's little army got up early in the morning and started toward the vast army of Midian. But the Lord told Gideon that his little army was too big!

"Send some of your men home,"

God said. "Tell anyone who is afraid to leave."

When Gideon told his men this, twenty-two thousand of them went home, while ten thousand stayed.

"There are still too many!" the Lord said. "Bring them down to the river, and I will choose the ones I want in the battle."

So Gideon brought them to the river. All the men were thirsty and began to drink. Some lifted the water to their mouths in their hands, and some stooped down and put their mouths into the water. The Lord said that only the ones who drank from their hands (there were three hundred of them) could go with him to the battle!

Gideon was afraid to go with so few, but the Lord told him to take one of his soldiers and creep over to the camp of the enemy through the darkness to listen to what they were saying.

The Midianites were as thick as grasshoppers in the valley below, and they had so many camels it was hard to count them. That night Gideon and another man crept down to their camp and listened outside one of the tents where two Midianite soldiers were talking. One was telling the other about a dream he had.

"In my dream," he said, "I saw a loaf of bread come tumbling into our camp; it struck against a tent and knocked it down flat on the ground!"

And the other man said, "Your dream means that the Lord is going to give Gideon a great victory over us!"

When Gideon heard this he went back to the three hundred men. He told them to get up and come with him, for the Lord would give them the victory. He put them in three different groups and gave each man a trumpet and a pitcher with a lighted lamp inside. He told them that when they came to the camp of the Midianites, they must do exactly as he did. When he blew his trumpet, they must all blow theirs and shout, "The sword of the Lord and of Gideon!"

In the middle of the night he and his three hundred men arrived in the camp of the Midianites. Suddenly he and all of his men blew their trumpets and broke the pitchers and shouted, "The sword of the Lord and of Gideon!"

When the Midianites heard the noise and saw the burning lamps that had been hidden in the pitchers, they yelled in fear and ran for their lives. The Lord made them afraid both of the men of Israel and of each other, too, so that they were killing and fighting one another all over the valley.

Gideon and his men chased them as they fled across the Jordan River. The two kings of the Midianites raced ahead of him with fifteen thousand soldiers. But he caught up with them and overcame them and took the two kings captive.

So the Midianites were driven out of Canaan, and the people of Israel were no longer their slaves.

Gideon was the judge of Israel for forty years. God gave him many sons, and he lived to be an old man.

QUESTIONS
What two miracles did God do for Gideon?
Why do you think God made Gideon's army so small?
How did they defeat the Midianites?

29
Samson's Riddle

A man named Samson now became Israel's leader. He went to a city called Timnath where he fell in love with a Philistine girl. She was not a Jewess, but when he returned home he told his father and mother about her and asked them to get her as his wife. His father and mother told him he should marry an Israeli girl, not a Philistine girl, for the Philistines were enemies of the Israelites. Besides, God had told His people not to marry non-Jews.

But Samson was not willing to give her up. He said to his father, "I want her, so get her for me."

His father and mother went back with him to Timnath. On the way there, a young lion came roaring out at Samson, and the Lord gave him strength to kill the lion with his hands as easily as if it had been a young goat.

When Samson finally met the girl and talked with her, he wanted all the more to marry her. A wedding date was set, and he and his parents went back home. When he returned to marry her, he came to the place where he had killed the lion and went over

to look at it. Its body was dried up, and a swarm of bees was living in it, storing honey there. He took some of the honey in his hands and ate it as he walked. Afterwards he gave some to his father and mother, but he didn't tell them he had taken it out of the dead body of the lion.

Samson gave a big party for the young men of the town, for that was one of the marriage customs of those days. Thirty Philistine youths came, and the party lasted seven days. During the party Samson decided to tell them a riddle. He promised to give each of the young men some fancy clothing if they found out what his riddle meant before the seven days of the party ended. But if they couldn't find the answer to his riddle, then each of them must give *him* a suit! The Philistine boys agreed to this bet.

"Go ahead," they said, "tell us the riddle."

"All right," Samson replied, "here it is: 'Food came out of the eater, and sweetness came out of the strong!'" (He meant that he had taken honey from a lion, and eaten it. But of course he didn't tell the Philistines the answer because then he would lose the bet!)

For three days they tried to find the answer, but couldn't. Finally the young men went to his bride and told her they would kill her and her whole family unless she found out from Samson the answer to the riddle.

She knew they would kill her, so she asked Samson to tell her, but he wouldn't. Then she started crying and saying he didn't love her or he would tell her.

"I haven't even told my father or my mother," Samson answered; "why should I tell you?"

But she kept on begging and crying, and he finally told her just to keep her quiet. Then of course she went and told the Philistine boys.

They came to Samson on the seventh day, just before the end of the feast, and pretended they had thought up the answer by themselves. "What is sweeter than honey?" they asked. "And what is stronger than a lion?" But Samson knew his wife had told them.

The Lord's time came for Samson to begin punishing the Philistines for their cruelty to the people of Israel. The Lord had told Samson's parents that their son would begin to free the Israelis from their slavery. That was why the Lord had made Samson strong enough to kill the young lion as easily as if it had been a baby goat.

Samson went to a Philistine city called Ashkelon and killed thirty men there. He took their clothes and gave them to the men at the wedding, to fulfill his promise of a suit to each of them if they found the answer to his riddle.

Then he left his wife and returned to his own home, while she stayed with her father in Timnath.

A few months later Samson went to visit her and to take her a present. But her father wouldn't let him in, because he had let another man marry her. Her father thought that Samson had gone away because he had decided he didn't want her. This was why he had given her to someone else.

Samson was very angry and went out and caught three hundred foxes. He tied burning torches to their tails and let them loose in the fields and vineyards of the Philistines, setting fire to their grain, grape vines and olive trees.

"Who has done this?" the Philistines demanded. When they knew it was Samson, they killed his wife and her father.

Then Samson took revenge by fighting against the Philistines and killing several of them. Afterward he camped on the top of a high rock in the land of Israel. The Philistines went there with an army of several thousand men to capture and kill him. But Samson picked up a donkey's jawbone that was lying by the road, and killed a thousand Philistines with it.

Afterward he was so tired he could hardly stand up. He prayed to the Lord, and the Lord opened a spring with water bubbling out; after Samson drank from it, his strength returned to him again.

He went to the city of Gaza and spent the night sleeping with a girl he had met. But this was wrong, for she was not his wife. This was a Philistine city and when the Philistines heard that Samson was there, they shut the city gates and watched all night to capture him when he went out again. But in the middle of the night he decided to leave town. When he found he couldn't leave because the gates were closed, he simply pulled the gate posts out of the ground, picked up the gates, put them on his shoulders, and carried them to the top of a nearby hill!

QUESTIONS
What animal did Samson kill with his hands?
How did the young men find the answer to the riddle?
Why did God make him so strong?
What else did Samson do with his great strength?

30
Samson and Delilah

One day Samson decided to visit a Philistine girl friend of his named Delilah. When the kings of the Philistine cities knew he was there, they promised to give Delilah eleven hundred pieces of silver if she would help them capture him. So Delilah begged Samson to tell her the secret of his great strength and how he could be made as weak as other men.

Samson told her a lie. He said that if he were tied with seven ropes made from green flax, then he would be as helpless as any other man.

Delilah told this to the kings of the Philistines, and she tied him with the ropes while he was asleep. He didn't know there were men hiding in the room to grab him.

When she had tied him up she cried out, "The Philistines are here

to get you, Samson!" Instantly, Samson woke up and broke the ropes as easily as if they were threads.

Delilah said he had mocked her and told her a lie and begged him to tell her the truth. How could he be tied up so that he couldn't get away? This time Samson said that if he were tied with two new ropes that had never been used before, he would not be able to break them. So she took two new ropes and tied him, while men hid in the room, then called out to him as before that the Philistines were coming to get him. But he broke the new ropes as easily as before.

Delilah scolded him for lying to her again, and again she begged him to tell her how to tie him so he couldn't get away. Samson said that if she would weave his long hair into a

Samson was so strong that he could break any ropes!

loom, his strength would leave him and he would be helpless. So she did this. But when she told him the Philistines were coming, he was as strong as ever.

"How can you say, 'I love you' when all you do is make fun of me and lie to me?" she asked. Day after day she begged him to tell her and would give him no rest. At last he told her the truth. He said that he had been a Nazirite since he was born. His hair had never been cut, and if it were, he would no longer be strong, but as weak as other men.

Why did Samson tell her this secret? He was telling her how to take away the strength the Lord had given him to fight against the enemies of Israel. He did it because he had chosen a girl for his friend who didn't care about God, and he listened to her until she persuaded him to do this great sin against God. You and I must be careful not to do wrong things even if people we like want us to and say we should. We must always listen to the Lord instead.

Delilah realized that this time Samson was finally telling her the truth. She sent this message to the kings of the Philistines: "Come once more; this time he has told me the truth!" So they came again and brought her the money they had promised.

Then, while Samson was asleep, a barber came and cut his hair.

Delilah woke Samson up and told him that the Philistines were coming to get him. He thought he could easily get away as he always had before, for he didn't realize that the Lord had let his strength go away. But this time the Philistines caught him, for he could no longer fight against them,

and they bound him with bronze chains. They poked out his eyes, making him blind, and shut him up in prison where they made him work very hard turning a millstone to grind their corn.

But while he was in prison, his hair began to grow longer again, and the Lord gave him back his strength.

One day the kings of the Philistines called the people together in their idol's temple to offer a sacrifice to their god Dagon and to rejoice because Samson had been caught. Everyone present praised Dagon because they thought he had helped them catch Samson! They were all very happy.

"Send for Samson so we can tease him," someone suggested. So they brought blind Samson out of the prison and set him between the two pillars that held up the roof of the temple and made fun of him there.

The temple was packed with people, including all the kings of the Philistines. Many of the people were having a party on the roof, while those inside the temple were laughing at Samson. A boy held him by the hand to lead him because he couldn't see. Samson asked the boy to place his hands on the pillars that held up the temple roof, so he could lean against them. The boy did.

Then Samson prayed, "O Lord, help me, and give me strength only this once." He gave a mighty push against the two pillars as he stood there between them, and said, "Let me die with the Philistines." As he pushed, the pillars moved apart, and the roof fell on the kings of the Philistines and on all the people inside, killing great numbers of them.

Samson died with them, but in his

death he killed more of the enemies of
Israel than he had while he was alive.
Then his brothers came and took his
dead body and buried it.

QUESTIONS
Why did Samson tell Delilah his secret?
What happened when Samson's hair was
    cut?
What did Samson do when God made
    him strong again?

R. Hook

31
The Story of Ruth

During the time judges ruled Israel, a man named Elimelech and his wife, Naomi, moved from Israel to the land of Moab.

His sons married Moabite girls, and they all lived together for about ten years. Then Elimelech and his two sons all died, leaving Naomi alone with her two daughters-in-law.

Naomi decided to go back to her home in the city of Bethlehem in Israel. She asked her daughters-in-law if they would rather stay in Moab, the land where they were born and where all their friends and relatives lived, or whether they wanted to move to Israel with her.

When her daughters-in-law learned of her decision to return to Israel, they cried. One of them, Orpah, decided to stay in Moab; but the other, Ruth, didn't want to leave Naomi.

"I'll go with you," she said, "and live wherever you live. Your friends will be my friends, and your God will be my God."

When Naomi saw how much her daughter-in-law Ruth loved her, she didn't urge her to stay in the land of Moab, but agreed to let her come with her to the land of Israel.

So they came to the city of Bethlehem where Naomi had lived before moving to Moab.

Her neighbors remembered her, of course, and the news of her arrival spread quickly. "Oh, there's Naomi!" they would exclaim. But she would reply, "No, don't call me Naomi anymore, for Naomi means 'pleasant.' Call me Mara, because that means 'bitter.' For the Lord has given me bitter troubles." She meant that when she left Bethlehem so many years before, her husband and her two sons were with her; but now all three were dead.

One day during harvest time, Ruth said to Naomi, "Let me go out to the harvest fields and pick up grain dropped by the harvesters." She said this because one of God's laws for His people was that poor people must always be allowed to pick up any bits of grain that dropped to the ground at harvest time. Ruth wanted to get some of this grain for them to eat.

Naomi agreed to this. Ruth went to a field belonging to a man named Boaz and began picking up the grains behind his workers.

When Boaz came out to the field

later that morning, he asked the foreman in charge of the reapers, "Say,
who is that girl over there?"

"She is the one who came with
Naomi from the land of Moab," the
foreman replied.

Boaz went over and talked to Ruth.
He was very pleasant to her and told
her to stay with his reapers and not
to go to some other field, for he had

warned his young men not to bother
her. When she was thirsty, he said
she should get water from the pitchers
placed there for his workers and drink
as much and as often as she wished.
And he told her to eat lunch with his
workers from the food he provided for
them.

Ruth thanked him very much and
asked him why he was so kind to her

since she was only a stranger. Boaz said it was because he knew about her kindness to her mother-in-law: how she had left her father and mother and the land where she was born, and had come to live among the people of Israel. He said he hoped God would bless her because she had done these things. He was glad, he said, that she had left the land of Moab where the people worshipped idols and had come to Canaan to worship the Lord.

Afterwards Boaz told his workers to drop some handfuls of grain on purpose so that she could find the grain and pick it up!

Ruth stayed in his field until evening, then beat out the barley grain she had gathered, and took it to her mother-in-law. When Naomi saw how much Ruth brought, she was glad, and asked the Lord to bless the man who had been so kind to her. She asked who it was, and Ruth said, "The man's name is Boaz." Naomi was surprised and told her he was a close relative of theirs! He was a very rich man, Naomi said.

Ruth said he had asked her to keep coming back to his field until the harvest ended. Naomi, too, said to do this; so Ruth went back day after day until the end of the harvest.

One day Naomi said to Ruth, "Boaz is threshing barley tonight at the threshing floor." In those days the grain was separated from the straw and chaff by throwing it up in the air while the wind was blowing. The wind would blow away the straw because it was so light, but the grain was heavier and would fall in a pile on the ground. A threshing floor was a smooth, level piece of ground where this was done. Naomi had heard that Boaz was to divide his barley from the chaff that night, and she had a plan! She told Ruth to go to the threshing floor and find Boaz. Then she told her what to say to him.

Ruth did as her mother-in-law said. Boaz and his workers winnowed his barley that night, and after a hearty supper he lay down for the night beside a stack of sheaves. When it was dark, Ruth went over and lay at his feet! Around midnight he woke up, startled and afraid. "Who's there?" he demanded.

"It's only me, sir," Ruth replied. Then she said what Naomi had told her to say. Because he was a close relative, she wanted him to take care of her and marry her.

The idea pleased him very much. "May the Lord bless you, my child," he replied. He said he would gladly marry her if he could, because all the people of Bethlehem knew what a fine person she was. But first he would need to talk with another man who was an even closer relative of Naomi's, who had the first right to marry her. If he didn't want to, then Boaz would. Boaz said he would talk to the other man that very day. So Ruth slept at his feet all night; and early the next morning before it was light, he gave her a large sack of barley to take home to Naomi. When she told Naomi what Boaz had said and showed her his present, Naomi told Ruth to be patient and see how it would all turn out.

That day Boaz called together ten of the city officials and told them that he wanted to marry Ruth. Soon, the other man who had the first choice of marrying her came by. He said he didn't want to marry Ruth, so Boaz

Ruth tries to comfort Naomi

could. Then all the city officials prayed that the Lord would bless Ruth and make Boaz still richer and greater than he was already.

So Boaz married Ruth, and Naomi was very happy. The Lord gave Boaz and Ruth a son, and grandmother Naomi loved the baby very much. They named the little boy Obed.

QUESTIONS

Why did Ruth go to Canaan with Naomi?

How was Boaz kind to Ruth?

Why was he pleased she had come to Canaan?

32

The Story of Jonah

Long ago Nineveh was one of the greatest cities in the world. In it there were temples and palaces, thousands of homes, beautiful gardens, and green fields for the cattle. Around the city were walls one hundred feet high. These walls were so thick that if there had been a road on top and automobiles in those days, three cars could have been driven along, side by side, on the top of this great wall. Fifteen hundred towers were built above the walls all around the city. These towers were each two hundred feet high. The Assyrian soldiers could shoot arrows from the walls at their enemies when they came to fight against Nineveh.

Nineveh was also a very wicked city. One day God spoke to the prophet Jonah and said, "Jonah, go to Nineveh, and tell the people about the punishment I am going to send them because of their sins."

But Jonah didn't want to go, so he ran away to Joppa, a city by the sea. There he found a ship headed in a different direction than Nineveh, so Jonah bought a ticket and got on board to try to get away from God.

When the ship had sailed out to sea, the Lord sent a strong wind and a great storm. The ship was in danger of sinking. The sailors were terrified and prayed for help, each one praying to his own god. Then they threw out some of the freight the ship was carrying, to make it lighter and to keep it from sinking. But Jonah didn't know the danger they were in, for he had gone down to the bottom of the ship and lay there fast asleep. The captain found him and woke him up.

"How can you sleep like this?" the captain shouted at him. "Get up and pray to your god; perhaps he may pity us and save us from dying."

Then the sailors talked together and said, "This storm has been sent because someone in the ship has been bad. Let's draw straws to find out whose fault it is."

They did, and Jonah drew the short one. They said to him, "Tell us, what wicked thing have you done? What country do you come from?"

Jonah replied, "I am a Hebrew, and I am running away from the God who made the sea and the dry land, because I don't want to obey Him."

Then the men were very much

afraid and said, "Why have you done this? What should we do to you so that the storm will stop?"

Jonah told them, "Throw me into the ocean; then it will become calm again. I know it is my fault that this danger has come upon you."

The men didn't want to throw him overboard and rowed hard to bring the ship to land, but they couldn't do it. They prayed to the God Jonah had told them about and cried out to Him, saying, "O Lord, please don't punish us for throwing this man into the ocean, for You have sent the storm because of him."

As soon as they had thrown Jonah in, immediately the sea grew still and calm. The men were amazed and offered a sacrifice to the Lord and promised to serve Him.

The Lord had sent a huge fish to

the side of the ship to swallow Jonah as soon as he fell in! Jonah stayed alive in the fish three days and three nights. He prayed to the Lord while he was in the fish and confessed his sin. God heard him and commanded the fish to swim to the shore and vomit him out.

Then the Lord spoke to Jonah a second time. "Go to Nineveh," He said, "and give the people My message."

So Jonah went to Nineveh. He walked through the city for many hours and finally came to the center and he shouted out God's message: "Forty days from now Nineveh will be destroyed because of the sins of its people."

When the king of Nineveh and the people heard this, they believed God had sent Jonah and they knew what he said would come true. The king took off his beautiful royal robes and wore cheap burlap instead. Then he and his government officials sent a message through the city commanding that no one could eat anything until further notice. "No man or animal," they said, "may eat any food or drink anything, and must wear rough burlap, and must pray with all his heart, and must stop being wicked. For who can tell? Perhaps the Lord will forgive us and take away His great anger from us and not destroy us after all."

God saw how they prayed to Him, and that they had stopped being bad, so He took away His punishment and didn't destroy the city after all.

QUESTIONS
Why was God going to punish the people of Nineveh?
Why did the sailors throw Jonah overboard?
How did God save Jonah?
What did the people of Nineveh do when they heard God was going to punish them?

33
A Little Boy Named Samuel

There was a man of Israel named Elkanah who lived in the city of Ramah. Every year he took a trip to the Tabernacle in Shiloh to sacrifice to God. His two wives, Hannah and Peninnah, always went with him. Elkanah loved Hannah more than Peninnah and gave her many presents. But Hannah was unhappy because Peninnah had children and she didn't, for the Lord hadn't given her any.

The giant fish throws up Jonah onto the shore

Samuel helps Eli, the High Priest

One day Hannah came to the Tabernacle and prayed. She promised the Lord that if He would give her a son, she would give him back to the Lord again, and he would be set apart to serve the Lord all his life at the Tabernacle.

Eli was the High Priest at the time. Hannah was crying as she prayed. Eli was sitting there and saw her lips moving but couldn't hear her speaking. For some reason he decided that she was drunk and was being silly or muttering to herself. He scolded her for it.

But Hannah told him, "Oh, no, sir, I am not drunk. I am praying in my heart to the Lord."

Then Eli spoke to her in a friendly way and told her he hoped God would give her what she was asking Him for. Then Hannah was glad.

The Lord answered Hannah's prayer and gave her a son. She named him Samuel, which means "Asked of God." She named him this because she had asked God for him and God had given him to her.

Soon after Samuel was born, the time came for his father to go to Shiloh again to sacrifice as he did each year. But Hannah didn't go this time; she wanted to wait until her little boy was older. Then she would take him with her and leave him at the Tabernacle to help God and His priests with their work, for this is what she had promised the Lord.

Finally the time came when he was old enough, and she took him to the Tabernacle.

"Do you remember me?" she asked Eli. "I am the woman who stood here praying to the Lord that time, and you thought I was drunk. I was praying for this child, and the Lord has given me what I asked for. Now I am giving him back to the Lord again; as long as he lives he shall be the Lord's." And so she left little Samuel at the Tabernacle to stay and help Eli.

Samuel helped Eli in any way he could. One night when Samuel had gone to bed, he heard a voice calling him.

"I'm here," he answered and jumped up and ran to Eli. "What do you want?" he asked him.

But Eli said, "No, I didn't call you; go back to bed." So he did.

But then Samuel heard the voice again, so again he ran to Eli and asked him, "Why are you calling me, Eli? What do you want?"

"I didn't call you, my son," Eli said, "Go and lie down again."

But Samuel heard the voice a third time and went to Eli and said, "I'm sure I heard you calling me. What do you want me to do?"

Then Eli knew it was the Lord who had called the child. He said to him, "Go, lie down; and if He calls you again say, 'Speak Lord, I am listening.'"

So Samuel went back to bed. And the Lord came and called as before, "Samuel, Samuel."

Samuel answered, "Yes, Lord, speak, for I am listening." Then the Lord told him He was going to punish Eli and his sons because his sons were so wicked, and Eli hadn't punished them.

QUESTIONS

Why was Hannah sad?

Why did she take Samuel to live at the Tabernacle?

Why were Eli's sons so bad?

34
David and Goliath

Once again the Philistine army decided to fight Israel, and Saul and the men of Israel got ready for the battle. The camp of the Philistines was on one mountain, and the camp of Israel was on another mountain; the two were separated by a valley

One of the Philistine soldiers was a giant named Goliath. He wore a lot of armor—a bronze helmet to protect his head, an armored coat, and sheets of bronze to cover his legs so that no sword or spear could wound him.

He strutted into the valley between the two armies and yelled to the army of Israel, "I'll fight the best man in your army. If he can kill me, we Philistines will be your slaves; but if I kill him, then you must be our slaves!"

Saul and the men of Israel were frightened; no one in Saul's army was willing to go out and fight with the giant. For forty days he came out every morning and evening to defy the men of Israel.

Meanwhile, David was feeding his father's sheep at Bethlehem, but his three oldest brothers were in Saul's army. One day David's father said to him, "Take this food to your brothers, and take this present of a cheese for their captain, and see how they are getting along."

Early in the morning David started out, leaving the sheep with one of his father's servants. He came to the camp of Israel just as the Israeli soldiers were getting ready for battle, and everyone was shouting and yelling.

David managed to find his brothers, and as he was talking to them, the giant, Goliath, strutted out and gave his usual taunt. When David heard everyone saying that there would be a huge reward for anyone who killed the giant, and he would be given the king's daughter as his wife, he decided to try for these prizes!

"How dare this giant defy the armies of the living God?" David demanded. When the men standing near him heard David say this, they realized that David wanted to fight Goliath. They told Saul, and Saul sent for him.

When David told King Saul that he would like to fight Goliath, King Saul objected.

"You can't possibly do it," he said. "Why, you're only a youngster, while Goliath has been a tough soldier for many years."

"But I can!" David answered. "One day while I was watching my

David defends his sheep

father's sheep, a lion grabbed a lamb and I went after it and struck the lion and he dropped the lamb. Then he came after me, but I caught him by his beard and killed him. Another time I killed a bear with my hands. And I'll do the same to this wicked giant, for he has defied the armies of the living God. The Lord who saved me from the jaws of the lion and the bear will save me from the sword of the giant."

"All right," Saul said, "go and fight him, and the Lord be with you."

Then Saul gave David his own armor—his bronze helmet, his armored coat, and his sword. But David said, "I'm not used to these," and took them off again.

He took his stick with him that he used to protect the sheep, and his slingshot. Choosing five smooth stones from the brook, he put them into his shepherd's bag, and started over toward Goliath. The giant saw him coming and rushed out to fight him. But when he saw David he didn't think he was worth fighting; for David didn't look like a strong, brave soldier, but like a shepherd boy who had never fought before.

"Am I a dog, that you come to me with a stick?" the giant asked angrily. And he called on the idols he worshipped to curse David. "Come over here so I can kill you," he yelled.

But David answered, "You come to me trusting in your sword, your shield, and your spear; but I come to you trusting in the God of Israel. Today He will give you to me, and I will kill you and cut off your head; and the army of the Philistines will be killed, and the birds and wild animals will eat them!"

As Goliath came closer, David ran toward him. Putting his hand into his shepherd's bag, he took out a stone, put it into his sling, and sent it sailing toward Goliath. It struck him square in the forehead, broke his skull, and he fell down dead. So David defeated the giant with a sling and a stone. David ran over to him and used Goliath's own sword to cut off his head.

When the Philistines saw that Goliath was dead they started to run. The army of Israel gave a great shout and started after them, killing many of them. Afterwards the men of Israel came back and went into the Philistines' camp and took all the gold, silver, and clothing from their tents.

David came from the battle with the head of Goliath in his hand. Then Abner, the captain of the army of Israel, took him to Saul.

"Who are you, young man?" Saul asked.

David answered, "I am the son of Jesse of Bethlehem." For some reason Saul didn't realize that this was the same boy who used to play the harp for him.

Saul's son Jonathan was there, and when he saw David and heard him speaking with his father, he loved him as a brother. Prince Jonathan was David's friend in all the troubles that lay ahead, and he and David promised always to be kind to each other.

Then Saul made David a captain in his army.

QUESTIONS
Who was Goliath?
How did David defeat him?

David fights the giant Goliath

35

A Dead Boy Lives Again!

A man named Ahab was now king of Israel. He was not a good king. In fact, he was very bad because he taught the people to worship idols instead of worshipping God. So God sent the prophet Elijah to tell Ahab that as punishment there would not be any more rain in the land of Israel for many years, until Elijah asked God to send it. Ahab was very angry with Elijah because God stopped the rain, and he wanted to kill Elijah, so the Lord told Elijah to go and hide.

"Go and hide beside a brook in the wilderness," the Lord said. "You can get drinking water from the brook, and I have commanded the ravens to feed you there!" So Elijah hid by the brook, and the ravens brought him food every morning and evening. But after awhile the brook dried up because there had been no rain, and a great famine came over the land.

Then the Lord said to Elijah, "Go to the city of Zarephath, for I have commanded a widow to feed you there."

When Elijah came to the gate of the city he saw a woman gathering sticks, and he called to her and said, "Please bring me a cup of water to drink." As she was going to get it he called to her again, and said, "And a piece of bread, too!"

But she answered, "As surely as God lives, I have no bread. I have only a handful of meal in a barrel, and a little olive oil in a bottle; and now I am gathering a few sticks to bake a little loaf of bread for me and my son to eat, and then we must die of starvation."

But Elijah told her "No, you won't! Go and bake the bread, but make a little loaf for me first, and bring it here, and there will be plenty left for you and your son! For the Lord says that although you have only a little flour and olive oil, it will last until the famine ends!"

She did as Elijah said, and sure enough, there was always olive oil left in the bottle and flour in the barrel, no matter how much she used! It was a wonderful miracle! This went on for a whole year until the famine ended.

One day the woman's son became

The ravens bring food to Elijah

sick and died. Elijah took him out of her arms and carried him up to his own room and laid him on his bed. Elijah pleaded with the Lord and said, "O Lord, why have You brought evil upon this woman in whose house I stay, by slaying her son? Please, O Lord, let the child live again!"

And the Lord heard Elijah's prayer, and the boy came back to life, and Elijah took him down to his mother. What a wonderful miracle!

QUESTIONS
Why did Elijah tell King Ahab about the weather?
How did Elijah get food and water when he was hiding?
What two miracles did God do for the widow?

36
Elijah Meets Baal's Prophets

There were many other prophets of the Lord besides Elijah in the land of Israel. But Queen Jezebel, the wicked wife of King Ahab, hated them all and tried to kill them.

Obadiah, the manager of Ahab's palace, was a good man who feared the Lord; so he hid a hundred of the Lord's prophets in caves where Jezebel couldn't find them, and sent them supplies of food and water.

After the famine had lasted for more than three years the Lord said to Elijah, "Go to King Ahab, and I will send rain."

King Ahab didn't know Elijah was coming, or that the Lord had promised rain, so King Ahab and Obadiah were out looking everywhere to find grass to save the horses and mules from dying of starvation. They went in different directions so they could finish their work faster.

As Obadiah was walking along, Elijah met him. Obadiah recognized him and said, "Are you Elijah, sir?"

"I am," Elijah replied. "Now go and tell King Ahab that I am here."

But Obadiah was afraid. "King Ahab has looked for you everywhere," he said, "and now as soon as I tell him you are here, the Lord will carry you away and hide you again, and when Ahab comes and can't find you, he will kill me."

But Elijah answered, "As surely as God lives, I will show myself to Ahab today."

So Obadiah found the king and told him, and he came to meet Elijah. When King Ahab saw Elijah he exclaimed, "There you are, you traitor." He said this because he blamed Elijah for the famine.

But Elijah answered, "I am not a traitor, but you and your family are, because you have forsaken the Lord and are worshipping Baal."

Then Elijah told King Ahab to send for all the people to come to Mount Carmel, and to bring with them all 450 of the priests of Ahab's idol, whose name was Baal. So all the people came with the priests.

Elijah asked the people, "How long will it be before you decide whether you will serve God or Baal? If the Lord is God, obey Him; but if Baal is God, then obey him."

The people heard what Elijah said, but didn't answer.

Elijah didn't know there were any other of the Lord's prophets left alive. He told the people that he was the only one in all the land, because all the rest had been killed or had run for their lives; but Baal had 450 prophets.

"Now bring two young bulls," Elijah said, "and let Baal's prophets kill one of them and lay it on Baal's altar, without any fire under it. And I will take the other young bull and kill it and lay it on the Lord's altar, without any fire under it. Then let them pray to Baal to send down fire from heaven to burn up their young bull. And I will pray to the Lord for fire to come from heaven to burn up the young bull on the altar of the Lord. Whichever god sends fire from heaven to burn up his offering, he is the real God." And all the people agreed.

Elijah prays to God for rain

Baal's prophets chose a young bull and killed it, and laid it on the wood on the altar, but put no fire under it. Then they cried out to their idol, Baal, from morning till noon.

"O Baal, hear us!" they shouted, and leaped up and down on their altar. But no voice answered them, and no fire came down from heaven to burn up their offering.

About noon, Elijah mocked them and said, "Call louder, for perhaps your god is talking to someone and isn't listening, or maybe he is away, or is asleep and must be awakened!"

So they yelled and shouted to Baal until evening, and cut themselves with knives until the blood gushed out, hoping it would attract Baal's attention and make him answer them. But no fire came.

Then Elijah gathered all the people around him and used twelve stones to rebuild the altar of the Lord that had long lain in ruins, and dug a trench around it. He put wood on the altar and cut the young bull apart and laid the pieces on the wood.

Then he said to the people, "Fill four barrels with water, and pour it over the sacrifice and over the wood." When they had done this, he said, "Do it a second time." And they did it a second time. "Now do it a third time," he said. And they did. So the water ran down over the sacrifice and over the wood, and filled the trench around the altar.

That evening, at the time when the priests at the Temple used to offer a lamb for a burnt offering, Elijah came near the altar and prayed to the Lord, saying, "Hear me, O Lord, hear me, so that these people will realize that You are the true God."

Then the fire of the Lord fell from heaven upon the altar and burned up the offering and the wood, and even the stones of the altar, and licked up the water in the trench.

When the people saw it, they all fell face downward to the ground, shouting, "The Lord, He is God! The Lord, He is God!"

And Elijah said to them, "Grab the prophets of Baal! Don't let a single one escape!" So the people arrested them and Elijah took them down to Kishon Brook and killed them there; for the Lord had commanded that anyone who told people to forsake God and to worship idols, must be executed.

QUESTIONS

How did Obadiah help the prophets of the Lord?

What test did Elijah suggest to prove who was God?

What happened when he prayed?

37

Daniel and a Dream

King Nebuchadnezzar of Babylon decided that he needed some new advisors, so he started a school to train some of the Israeli boys who had been captured at Jerusalem. He said that all the students at the school must be handsome, quick to learn, and in perfect health. He wanted them to learn everything there was to know. They would attend his school for three years, and then would work for the king as his advisors and government officials.

Among those chosen to go to school were four Jewish boys whose names were Daniel, Shadrach, Meshach, and Abednego. These young men had a problem: they loved God and wanted to obey Him, but the king didn't want them to. The king said that they should pray to idols before every meal and thank them for the food. But God said no. So what should they do?

Daniel and his three friends decided to ask the king for permission to eat other food, instead of food for which the idols had been thanked.

Daniel talked to one of his teachers about it. This man liked Daniel a lot, but he didn't dare give permission. "I'm afraid it will make the king angry," he said. "If he notices that you

look paler and thinner than the young men who eat the food blessed by the idols, he will be angry with me and kill me."

"Please let us try it for just ten days," Daniel begged. "Give us only vegetables and water, and after ten days see if we don't look as well as the fellows who eat the other food. If we don't, then we will go ahead and eat the same as the others do."

The teacher finally agreed, and they were fed vegetables and water for ten days. At the end of that time they looked better and healthier than any of the others! So from then on they could eat whatever they wanted to. God helped them become wise, and he made Daniel able to understand the meaning of dreams.

At the end of their three years' training, the teachers brought them to the palace. There King Nebuchadnezzar talked with them and soon realized that these four Jewish boys were the best students of all! They always knew the right answers when the king was puzzled, and the king discovered that they were ten times smarter than the wisest men in his kingdom.

One night King Nebuchadnezzar

wakened from a dream and couldn't get back to sleep. So he summoned all his wise men, and they came and stood before him. "I had a dream that worries me," he said.

"Well," the wise men replied, "tell us the dream and we will tell you what it means."

But the king said, "I can't remember it! And if you won't tell me what I was dreaming about, and what it means, you will be killed and your houses torn down and made into piles of ruins. But if you tell me my dream and what it means, you'll be the richest, most honored men in the kingdom."

"But you have to tell us the dream before we can tell you what it means!" they protested. "Why, there isn't a man on earth who can tell a person what he dreamed about, and no king or ruler would even think of asking such a thing. Only the gods could tell you, and they don't live on earth."

Then the king was very angry and ordered all of them killed because they hadn't told him his dream!

Daniel and his three friends hadn't been summoned before the king, but they were among the wise men, so the king's death order for all the wise men meant that they would be killed too. But when a soldier came to kill them, Daniel asked what it was all about, and when he found out, he said to quit killing people and he would tell the king what he had dreamed!

Then Daniel went home and told his three friends to pray and ask God to show him what the king's dream was, so that they wouldn't be killed. And that night, in a vision, God showed the dream to Daniel.

Then Daniel praised God, and said,

"I thank You and praise You, O God of my fathers, because You have heard our prayer, and have told me what the king wants to know."

Then Daniel went to the captain of the king's bodyguard and said to him, "Don't kill the wise men of Babylon, but take me to the king and I will tell him the meaning of his dream."

So the captain rushed Daniel before the king, and the king said to him, "Can you tell me my dream and its meaning?"

Daniel replied, "The wisest man on earth can't tell it to the king; but there is a God in heaven who tells secrets: and God has told me what your dream was, not because I am wiser than anyone else, but so that you will know that He is the true God. He has told you in your dream what will happen in the future."

Then Daniel told King Nebuchadnezzar his dream: "You saw a great statue of a cruel king, gleaming in the sunlight.

"Its head was made of gold, its chest and arms of silver, the rest of its body of brass; its legs were iron, and its feet were part iron and part clay. As you watched, a stone cut without hands from a mountain cliff struck the feet of the statue and shattered them. Then the statue crashed to the ground and the iron, the brass, the silver, the gold, and the clay were all broken small as dust, and the wind blew it all away. Afterwards, the stone that had broken the statue grew to be a great mountain and filled all the earth. That was your dream."

Then Daniel told the king what the dream meant:

The gold, silver, brass, iron, and clay meant different kingdoms. The head of gold meant Nebuchadnezzar himself, because God had given him the greatest of the kingdoms, making him greater than any other king in all the earth. But after he died, new world powers would rise, represented by the silver, brass, iron, and clay. And last of all, the Lord would set up one more kingdom which would never be destroyed. It would smash all the other kingdoms just as the stone cut from the mountain had broken the statue in Nebuchadnezzar's dream. This stone meant the kingdom of Christ that would someday come upon all the earth.

After Daniel told the king the dream and its meaning, the king threw himself to the ground in front of Daniel to show him deep respect, and said to him, "Your God is a God of gods and a King of kings and can tell secrets, for He has told you this dream."

Then the king made Daniel a great man and gave him gifts and appointed him ruler over the province of Babylon, and he became the head of the wise men. And at Daniel's request, his three friends became rulers too.

QUESTIONS
Do you remember what problem Daniel and his friends had?
Why do you think they looked healthier than everyone else without eating meat?
Could any wise man know what the king dreamed?
What did Nebuchadnezzar's dream mean?

38

Three Boys in a Furnace

King Nebuchadnezzar of Babylon now made a huge statue of gold and set it on a plain in the province of Babylon. Then he sent for all of his princes, governors, captains, judges, and all the other rulers of his kingdom to come and worship it. One of the king's assistants told them, "It is commanded that as soon as the band begins to play, you must fall down and worship Nebuchadnezzar's gold statue. If anyone refuses, he shall be thrown into a flaming furnace."

Then the king commanded the band to begin to play and instantly everyone fell down and worshipped the gold statue.

Daniel's three friends refused to do it, because they knew it was wrong to worship a statue. Then some of the Babylonians went to the king and complained to him about them.

Three men were thrown in the furnace—but who is the fourth?

"Didn't you make a law that every-one must fall down and worship the statue when the band begins to play, and that if anyone refuses, he will be tossed into a white-hot furnace?" they asked him. "Well, there are some Jews holding high political positions in your empire, and these men haven't obeyed you; they don't worship your gods, and they refuse to bow to your gold statue. They are Shadrach, Me-shach, and Abednego."

King Nebuchadnezzar was furious. He commanded that the three young men be arrested at once and brought to him. "Is it true, O Shadrach, Me-shach, and Abednego," he shouted, "that you do not worship my gods, and refuse to bow to my gold statue? I'll give you one more chance. When you hear the band begin to play, *fall down and worship the statue,* or you will be thrown at once into a flaming furnace; and who is the god who will be able to save you from my anger?"

Then Shadrach, Meshach, and Abednego said to the king, "We won't do it! If you throw us into the fur-nace, our God is able to save us, and He will. But even if He doesn't, we will not worship your gods, sir, nor bow to your gold statue."

Nebuchadnezzar's fury became more fierce. "Heat the furnace seven times hotter than ever before!" he commanded his men. Then he called for the biggest soldiers in his army to tie up Shadrach, Meshach, and Abed-nego and throw them in. The furnace was so hot that the flames killed the soldiers, but after Shadrach, Meshach, and Abednego had fallen down into the fire inside the furnace, they got up again and walked around in the flames! For God wouldn't let them be burned. The only things that burned were the ropes they were tied with; these burned from their wrists!

King Nebuchadnezzar was sur-prised beyond belief when he saw the three boys walking around in the fire! "Didn't we throw three men into the fire, tied tightly with ropes?" he ex-claimed. "And now there are four of them, loose and walking around in the fire! And the fourth looks like the Son of God!"

Nebuchadnezzar got as near as he could to the mouth of the furnace and shouted to them, "Shadrach, Meshach, and Abednego, you servants of the Most High God, come out!"

So out they came. The princes, gov-ernors, and captains crowded around them and could see that the fire hadn't hurt them a bit; not a hair of their heads was even singed, and they didn't even smell of smoke!

Then Nebuchadnezzar said, "Bless-ed be the God of Shadrach, Meshach, and Abednego, who has sent His angel and saved these young men who trusted in Him. Therefore I now make a law that anyone who says anything bad about the God of Shadrach, Me-shach, and Abednego shall be de-stroyed, and his house shall be torn down and made into a heap, for there is no other God that can rescue people as their God can!" Then the king made Shadrach, Meshach, and Abed-nego even greater than they had been before.

QUESTIONS

Why did Shadrach, Meshach and Abed-nego make Nebuchadnezzar angry?

What happened when they were thrown into the furnace?

What did Nebuchadnezzar do after-wards?

39

Daniel in the Lions' Den

King Darius of Babylon decided to divide the empire into 120 states ruled by 120 governors. Over these governors were three presidents, with Daniel as their chief because of the wise and good spirit that was in him. Darius was planning to make Daniel ruler over the entire empire. But when the other presidents and governors heard about it, they were jealous and tried to find something bad to say about him to the king. But they couldn't find a thing, for he was faithful to his duties and they couldn't point out a single fault. Finally they decided, "We'll never be able to complain about Daniel to the king except possibly about his religion."

So they came to the king, and said, "King Darius, live forever! All the presidents and governors of your kingdom want a law made that any person who prays to anyone but you for the next thirty days shall be thrown into a den of lions. O king, make this law and sign it, so that even you can't change it." And King Darius signed the law.

When Daniel knew that the law was signed, he went home, opened the windows of his room toward Jerusa-lem, knelt, and prayed and gave thanks to God three times a day, just as he always had done before. Then the other presidents and governors got together and went over to Daniel's house and found him praying, and rushed back to the king and said, "Didn't you make a law that any person praying to anyone but you for thirty days must be thrown into the den of lions?"

"Yes," the king said, "I certainly did. It is now a law of the Medes and Persians which can never change."

Then they said, "That fellow Daniel isn't obeying you, O king, for he prays to his God three times a day!"

The king was crushed! Oh, why had he signed that law? He didn't want to punish Daniel. He tried every way he could to save him. But the presidents and the governors said to him, "You know perfectly well, O king, that no law the king has signed can be changed!"

So at last King Darius gave up, and Daniel was thrown into the den of lions. But first the king said to him, "O Daniel, your God whom you serve so faithfully will save you."

Then, after Daniel was thrown in,

a great stone was rolled across the mouth of the lions' den so that no one could get Daniel out.

The king went home to his palace and refused to eat, and sent away the orchestra that played for him each evening. He was up very early the next morning and hurried out to the lions' den, and called sadly to Daniel: "O Daniel, servant of the living God, was this God of yours able to deliver you from the lions?"

Then Daniel called to the king, "O king, my God has sent His angel to shut the lions' mouths so that they haven't even scratched me!"

The king was overcome with joy and excitement and commanded that Daniel be taken out at once. So Daniel was unhurt because he trusted in his God.

QUESTIONS
Do you think Daniel was right when he refused to obey Darius?
Why wasn't Daniel hurt by the lions?

40

Beautiful Esther

Not all the Jews went back to Jerusalem with Zerubbabel and Ezra; many of them still lived in the land of Persia. King Ahasuerus was now the Persian emperor. In the third year of his reign he prepared a great party for his officers in the garden court of his palace, in the city of Shushan where the kings of Persia lived during the winter. The courtyard of the palace was decorated with white, green, and blue curtains. The benches in the courtyard were made of gold and silver, and the pavement was red, blue, white, and black marble. Those invited to the party drank from cups of gold, and there was plenty of wine for everyone to drink as much as he wanted.

Queen Vashti held a party at the same time for the women who lived and worked in the palace of King Ahasuerus. On the seventh day of the king's party, when he was drunk, he sent for Queen Vashti, to show everyone her beauty. In Persia the women lived in a separate part of the house, by themselves, and never came out before men unless they wore veils. So when King Ahasuerus sent for Queen Vashti to come before all the princes and people with her face unveiled, she refused knowing that this would be quite wrong.

But the king was so angry at her refusal that he called in his advisors and asked them, "What shall I do to Queen Vashti? How shall she be punished for not obeying me?"

One of the men replied, "Vashti has done wrong not only to you but to all the people of your kingdom. All the women of Persia will stop obeying their husbands when they hear that you commanded Queen Vashti to come and she refused. Let the king make a decree, and let it be written among the laws of the Medes and Persians which cannot be changed, that Queen Vashti shall never see the king again; and let the king choose someone else for his queen. Then, when this becomes known, wives everywhere will be afraid not to obey their husbands."

The king and his aides thought this was a good idea. So he sent letters through all the different provinces of his kingdom, commanding every husband to make his wives obey him.

Then the king's advisors said to him, "Let's have a national beauty contest to discover the most beautiful girls in Persia. Bring them all here to the palace to become your wives, and the one you decide you like best will be the new queen instead of Vashti." So that is what they did.

Among the government officials at the palace there was a Jew named Mordecai who had a young cousin named Esther. She was a Jewess. Her father and mother had died, so Mordecai adopted Esther as his daughter and brought her up in his house. She was very beautiful, so she was selected to be one of the king's new wives. But would she be the one selected as his queen? Everyone liked Esther very much and hoped she would be the one he would choose. She was given seven young girls to wait on her and was given a nice apartment in the harem, the place where the king kept his wives.

But Esther didn't tell anyone she was a Jewess, for Mordecai had advised her not to.

Sure enough, King Ahasuerus loved Esther more than any of the other girls who were brought to him, so he placed the royal crown upon her head and made her queen instead of Vashti. Then the king celebrated with a big party and gave gifts to all his servants.

QUESTIONS
How did the king find a new queen?
Why didn't Esther tell anyone she was a Jewess?

41

Evil Haman Makes a Law

It so happened that two of the king's officers were angry with the king and wanted to kill him. Mordecai heard them talking and discussing their plans. He sent a message to Esther, telling her about the danger the king was in, and Esther told the king. The men were arrested and executed by being hanged on a gallows. Mordecai's deed in saving the king's life was written down in a book that told about all the main things that happened while he was king.

There was a man at the palace named Haman who was very great, for he was in charge of all the king's assistants. They all bowed to him, for the king had told them to. But Mordecai wouldn't do it. They asked Mordecai, "Why don't you obey the king and bow to Haman?" They kept asking him about this for several days, but he wouldn't listen to them, so they finally told Haman about it.

When Haman realized that Mordecai wasn't bowing to him, he was very angry and determined to punish him. But he wasn't satisfied to punish Mordecai alone; he decided that since Mordecai was a Jew, he would punish all the Jews of Persia.

So Haman said to King Ahasuerus, "There are people called Jews scattered all through your kingdom, and they have laws of their own which are different from our laws; and they don't obey the king's laws. It is not good to let such people live. If the king will make a law to have them all killed, I will pay a hundred thousand dollars into the king's treasury."

King Ahasuerus agreed to this. He told Haman to make any law he wanted to against the Jews, and he would sign it.

Then Haman wrote a law declaring that on the thirteenth day of February the people of Persia were to kill all the Jews in the kingdom, both young and old—women and children as well as men and boys. Whoever killed a Jew could have that Jew's house and money for himself. Haman sealed the decree with the king's ring, and copies of it were sent by messengers to the governors and rulers of all the provinces, so that all the people of Persia would know about it.

When Mordecai heard about the law Haman had made, he was filled with horror; he tore his clothes, and

put on sackcloth and went out into the streets of the city and cried with a loud and bitter cry. And in every province where the messengers brought the decree, there was great mourning among the Jews, and going without food, and weeping.

Queen Esther hadn't heard about this new law, but her maids came and told her that Mordecai was clothed in sackcloth, and crying out in the street. This made Esther sad, and she sent new clothes to him, but he wouldn't take them. So Esther called one of the king's assistants and sent him to ask Mordecai what the trouble was. Mordecai told him all that had happened, and about the money Haman had promised to pay into the king's treasury if the king would let him kill the Jews. Mordecai gave him a copy of Haman's law to show to Esther; and he asked him to tell the queen to go to the king and beg him to spare the lives of the Jews.

When he told Esther what Mordecai said, Esther sent back this message: "Everyone knows that anyone going to the king without being sent for will be killed instantly unless the king holds out his golden sceptre. And he hasn't sent for me to come to him during the last four weeks. How can I go and speak with him?"

But Mordecai returned this message to Esther: "Don't think that our enemies will spare you just because you are the queen, when they kill all the other Jews. If you don't try to save your people now, someone else will do it, but you and I and all your relatives will die. And who knows, perhaps God made you queen for just this purpose, to help the Jews at this particular time?"

Then Esther sent word to Mordecai, "Gather together all the Jews in this city, and tell them to go without food and pray for me. Do not eat or drink for three days, night or day; I and my maidens will do the same. Then I will try to go in and speak with the king. And if I die, I die."

So Mordecai called all the Jews together, and they did as Esther commanded.

QUESTIONS

How did Mordecai help the king?
Why did Haman make the law about the Jews?
What did Mordecai ask Esther to do?
What did he do to help her?

Esther goes to speak with the king

42

Brave Esther Saves the Jews

Three days later Queen Esther dressed herself in her royal robes and went into the inner part of the king's palace and stood before the king as he sat upon his throne. And God was with her, for the king held out his golden sceptre to her. So she came to him, and touched the top of the sceptre.

Then the king asked her, "What is it you wish, Queen Esther? Whatever it is I will give it to you, even if it is half of my kingdom."

Esther answered, "Please come today with Haman to a banquet I have prepared for you!"

Then the king said to his aides, "Tell Haman to hurry and get ready."

So the king and Haman came to the banquet. The king knew Esther wanted to ask some favor from him, and so as they sat at the banquet he asked her again, "What is it you wish? I will give it to you, even if it is half of my kingdom."

Esther answered, "Please come with Haman to another banquet I will prepare for you tomorrow, and then I will tell you what it is I want to ask of you."

Haman was thrilled and proud to be invited—he and no one else except the king himself—but as he was leaving the palace he noticed Mordecai sitting at the gate refusing to bow to him. He was very angry, but said nothing.

When he arrived home, he called for his friends and for his wife, and boasted to them of his riches and greatness, and told them how the king had honored him above all the princes, and above all the king's other aides.

"Yes," he said, "and Queen Esther invited no one else but me and the king to come to her banquet. And tomorrow I am invited again, with the king! Yet I can't be happy while I see Mordecai the Jew sitting there refusing to bow to me."

Then his wife and all his friends said, "Make a gallows seventy-five feet high, and tomorrow ask the king for permission to hang Mordecai on it; then you can be happy at the queen's banquet."

Haman was pleased with this advice, and he had the gallows made that very afternoon.

That night the king couldn't sleep. He told his servants to bring him the history book recounting the principal events of his reign. So the book was brought to him and as he was reading from it he noticed the item about how Mordecai had saved his life. For Mordecai had told him about the plot against his life.

King Ahasuerus asked his aides, "What reward or honor was given to Mordecai for this?"

"Nothing, sir," they replied.

While the king was talking about this, Haman arrived at the palace to ask the king for permission to hang Mordecai on the gallows. When the king was told that Haman was outside and wanted to see him, he said, "Yes, tell him to come in."

So Haman came in, and before he had a chance to tell the king his errand, the king said to him, "Haman, what is the highest honor I can give to a man who has helped me?"

Haman said to himself, "The king must mean me: I am the one he wants to honor."

So he said, "Let the man wear the king's robes, and his crown, and let him ride upon the king's horse; and let one of the king's most noble princes lead the horse through the streets of the city and shout to all the people, 'See how the king is honoring this man!'"

"Good!" the king said to Haman. "Take these robes of mine and get my personal horse, and take the crown, and do as you have said, to Mordecai the Jew."

Well, Haman had no choice but to obey the king, so he took the king's robes, his horse, and his crown, and brought them to Mordecai, and led him on horseback through the streets of the city, shouting out to all the people, "This man is being honored by the king!"

Afterwards Mordecai returned quietly to his duties at the king's gate, while Haman hurried home, full of shame, hiding his face so that no one would recognize him. As he was telling his wife and friends what had happened, the king's messenger arrived to take him to Queen Esther's banquet.

There at the banquet the king asked Esther again, "What is your wish, Queen Esther? What is your request? For it shall be given you, even to the half of my kingdom."

Esther answered, "If the king is pleased with me, this is my request, that the king will save my life and the lives of all the Jews. For we face death. I and all my people are to be killed; every one of us must die."

"Who would dare to touch you and your relatives?" King Ahasuerus roared.

Esther answered, "This wicked Haman is our enemy."

Haman turned pale with fright as the king rose from the table in great fury and stalked out into the palace garden. When he came in again, Haman had fallen down beside the queen to beg for his life. But the king had decided to kill him.

"Why not hang him on the gallows made for Mordecai?" someone suggested.

And the king said, "Yes, hang him there." So that is the way Haman died.

King Ahasuerus gave Haman's palace to Queen Esther, and Mordecai was called in before the king (for Esther now told the king that Mordecai was her cousin, and how kind he had been to her) and the king appointed him as his prime minister, the job Haman had had before.

Then Esther went to the king again,

though he had not called for her, and fell down crying at his feet. The king held out the golden sceptre toward her and she stood before him and begged that Haman's law dooming all the Jews be changed. "For how can I bear to see my people die?" she wept.

But even the king couldn't change it, for no law of the Medes and Persians could ever be changed, not even by the king himself. Then King Ahasuerus had an idea! He told Esther and Mordecai to make another law giving the Jews permission to fight back against anyone who tried to harm them!

Mordecai sent copies of this new law to all the provinces of the kingdom. The message went by swift messengers on horseback, mules, camels,

and young dromedaries.

So on the thirteenth day of February the Jews gathered together in every city, armed to fight for their lives; and they destroyed all their enemies. So God saved Esther and her people from those who had tried to destroy them. Then Esther and Mordecai sent letters to all the Jews telling them to hold an annual celebration of their victory, with parties and presents for each other and for the poor.

QUESTIONS
Why do you think Esther gave two banquets?
How do you think Haman felt when the king honored Mordecai?
What happened to Haman?
How did the king help the Jews?

43
God's Special Messenger

Now the time came for the Saviour to arrive on earth. And how the world needed Him, for everyone was selfish and unhappy! No one was pleasing to God. All the people in the world were sinners, just as Adam and Eve had been. When Adam and Eve sinned in the Garden of Eden, God promised them that a Saviour would come someday to take away their sins. The prophets too had often told the people

of Israel that this wonderful Saviour was going to come.

One day the time came, and God sent His angel to Mary. She was a Jewish girl who was a relative of King David, who had lived hundreds of years before. She was frightened, for she had never seen an angel before. But Gabriel said, "Don't be afraid, Mary! God has greatly blessed you. You are going to have a baby and His

The angel talks with Mary

name will be JESUS. He will have no human father, for He will be the Son of God. And God is giving a baby to Zacharias and your cousin Elizabeth."

Mary didn't understand how she would have a baby, for she was a virgin, that is, she wasn't married and so she had never slept with a man. But the angel explained that this wasn't necessary, for God would do a special miracle to make her pregnant while she was a virgin. No other baby has ever been born without a human father. Jesus was different. How ex-

cited and happy Mary was at this wonderful news that she would be the mother of the Saviour of the world!

She was engaged to be married to a kind man named Joseph, who was a carpenter. But when he heard that Mary was going to have a baby, he was sad. He thought she had sinned and that some other man was the baby's father. He said that now he wouldn't marry her. But God talked to him about it and explained that God was the baby's father, so it was all right for him to marry her after all; so he did. But he didn't sleep with her until after her baby, Jesus, was born.

QUESTION
What did Gabriel tell Mary?

44

The Birth of God's Son

In those days the Jews were under the rule of the Romans; they had to do whatever the emperor of Rome and his assistants told them to. Now he made a law that the name and address of every Jew must be written down. He instructed everyone to go to the city where his ancestors had lived, so that the Roman officers could record their names. Ancestors means relatives who lived hundreds of years before. So Joseph and Mary went to Bethlehem where King David used to live, because they were relatives of his, though he had lived hundreds of years before they were born.

But when they arrived at Bethlehem there was no room for them at the little hotel; it was already full. So they went out to the stable where the donkeys and camels were kept, to sleep in the straw on the floor. And while they were resting in the stable, Mary's baby was born. He was the little son that the angel Gabriel had told her about. Yes, Jesus was born out there in the stable; and Mary dressed Him in some baby clothes she had brought, and wrapped Him up in a blanket, and laid Him in a manger.

That same night some shepherds in the fields outside the town were watching their sheep to protect them from wild animals. Suddenly an angel surrounded by a bright light appeared to them. They were very frightened. But the angel said, "Don't be afraid; for I have good news for you, and for all the world! Tonight, in Bethlehem, your Saviour was born! His name is Christ the Lord.

"And this is how you will know Him: you will find Him wrapped in baby clothes and lying in a manger!"

Then suddenly many, many other angels appeared, praising God and saying, "Glory to God! Peace on earth between God and men!"

After the angels returned to heaven the shepherds said to each other, "Let's hurry to Bethlehem and find the baby!" So they ran into the village and soon found Mary and Joseph, and the baby lying in a manger! Afterwards the shepherds returned to their flocks again, praising God for what they had seen and heard.

When the baby was eight days old, his parents named Him Jesus, just as the angel Gabriel had told them to.

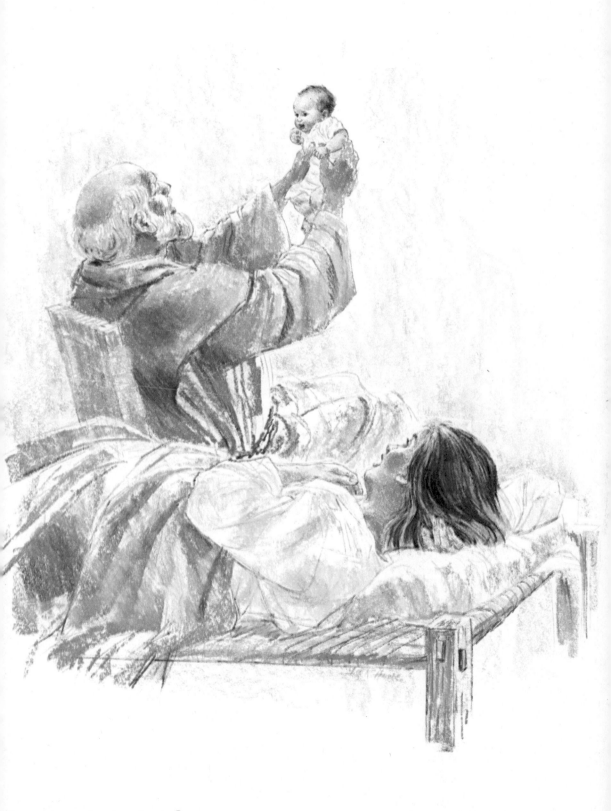

John the Baptist is born

And they dedicated Him to the Lord, for He was the Son of God.

Then Joseph and Mary took Him from His home in Bethlehem to the Temple at Jerusalem, and sacrificed young pigeons as the law required for the oldest boy in every Jewish family. And there he was circumcised. Circumcision is a tiny operation of cutting away the loose skin around the tip of the penis. God had commanded this to be done to all Jewish baby boys.

There was a wonderful old man named Simeon there at the Temple that day who loved God very much, and had been waiting many years to see the Saviour whom God had promised to send. The Holy Spirit had promised Simeon that he would not die before seeing Jesus. So, on the day Jesus' parents took Him to the Temple, the Holy Spirit told Simeon to go there, and when Joseph and Mary brought in their baby, Simeon took Him in his arms and said, "Now, Lord, Your promise has come true: I have seen the Saviour. Now I can die in peace."

Also at the Temple that day was a very old woman named Anna. She was a prophetess, that is, God sometimes told her about things that would happen in the future. She was a widow, and for many years had lived near the Temple so that she could worship there at any time, day and night. While Simeon was holding the baby Jesus in his arms and talking to Mary and Joseph, Anna came in and saw them there, and began thanking God for letting her see God's Son.

Not long afterwards some men who study the stars came to Jerusalem from a distant eastern land. "Where is the baby who will become king of the Jews?" they asked. "For we have seen His star and have come to worship Him." They knew in some way from seeing the star that Jesus had been born. So they came to Jerusalem looking for Him, but they didn't know just where to search.

When King Herod heard them asking about a new king, he was worried, for he was the king and he didn't want anyone else to have his job! He told the men to find Jesus, and then to come and tell him where He was so that he could worship Jesus too! But what he really intended was to kill Jesus.

King Herod now summoned some priests who had spent their lives studying the Scriptures, and asked them whether the Bible said where the new king would be born.

"Yes," they replied, "in the city of Bethlehem; that is what one of the prophets said."

So Herod sent the astrologers to Bethlehem. "Go to Bethlehem and search for the child," he said, "and when you have found him, come and tell me so that I can worship him too!"

So the men went to Bethlehem. And as they went, the star they had seen appeared to them again, and seemed to stand right over one certain house. They went in and saw the baby there with His mother Mary, and they bowed low before Him, worshipping Him. Then they gave presents to the new king—precious gifts of gold and spices. Afterwards they returned to their own country, but they didn't go through Jerusalem, for in a dream God warned them not to tell Herod where Jesus was.

Jesus is born in a stable

The shepherds are told about Jesus by an angel

Simeon holds the baby Jesus

Gifts from far away for Jesus

When Herod discovered that the astrologers had disobeyed him, he was very angry and sent his soldiers to Bethlehem to kill all the little children two years old or less. Since he didn't know which baby was the little king, he killed them all. But before the soldiers arrived, the angel of the Lord told Joseph to hurry to Egypt with the baby and His mother. So Joseph wakened them in the night and they fled to Egypt and stayed there until King Herod was dead. Then the angel spoke to Joseph again and told him, "Go back to the land of Israel, for King Herod is dead."

Joseph did as the angel commanded, and he and Mary and Jesus came and lived in the city of Nazareth.

QUESTIONS

Why did Mary and Joseph go to Bethlehem?

What did the angels tell the shepherds?

How do you think Simeon and Anna knew that Jesus was the promised Savior?

How did the astrologers know where to look for Jesus?

What terrible thing did Herod do?

Mary and Joseph take Jesus to Egypt

Jesus grows up

45

Jesus Grows Up

Joseph and Mary went to Jerusalem every year to celebrate the Passover. When Jesus was twelve years old, he went with them. After the celebration ended, they started walking back to their home in Nazareth, along with many other people. For friends and neighbors travelled together to the celebrations at Jerusalem. Some rode on mules and horses, but many of them walked. Joseph and Mary noticed that Jesus wasn't with them, but thought He was with some of their friends, so they didn't worry. But when they didn't see Him all day, and evening came and still He wasn't back, they began looking for Him and worrying, and asking everyone if they had seen Him. But no one had. By this time they were *very* worried and started back to Jerusalem to search for Him there. It took them a day to return and it was another day before they finally found Him. He was at the Temple talking with the great teachers there, listening to them and asking them questions!

These men were greatly surprised at how much Jesus knew, for He was only twelve years old, while they were college professors.

"Son!" His mother exclaimed, "why have You treated us like this? Your father and I have been searching for You everywhere."

Jesus was surprised. "Didn't you know I would be here at the Temple?" He asked.

Joseph and Mary didn't understand what He meant, but His mother always remembered what He had said and often thought about it. Afterwards she understood—He was the Son of God and naturally would want to be at His Father's house, which was the Temple.

Then Jesus returned home to Nazareth with His parents and did all that they told Him to do. And as He grew, God blessed Him; and everyone loved Him.

The next we are told about Jesus, He was a man thirty years old. But very few knew that He was the Son of God, for John the Baptist hadn't yet begun to tell them about Him.

Meanwhile John was living out in the wilderness. His clothes were wov-

Jesus talks with the priests in the temple

en of coarse camel hair, fastened around his waist by a leather belt. He ate locusts for his food—they were plentiful out there in the wilderness —and honey from the wild bees.

But now the time had come for John to preach to the people, telling them to get ready for the Saviour by turning from their sins. He began his preaching beside the Jordan River, and great crowds came there to hear him. He told them that the Saviour would soon be coming to save them and to destroy the wicked. John said that they mustn't think their sins would be forgiven just because they were descended from a good man like Abraham! No, they themselves must obey God. Many who heard John preach turned from their sins and were baptized by him in the river.

Then Jesus came to John and asked to be baptized. John didn't want to do it. *"I need to be baptized by You,"* John told Him; "why do You come to me?" Jesus had no sins to be washed away; why then should He be baptized? It was because He had come to earth to obey all of God's commandments for us.

Jesus told John to baptize Him anyway, even though he didn't understand why, for it was necessary. So John agreed. Then, as Jesus was coming up out of the water after being baptized, the sky above Him opened and what looked like a dove came down from heaven and lighted upon Him. It was the Holy Spirit. At the same time God's voice spoke from heaven saying, "This is My beloved Son. I am very pleased with Him."

Afterwards Jesus went out into the wilderness alone for forty days and forty nights. All that time He ate nothing, but fasted and prayed to God; and afterwards He was hungry.

Do you remember how Satan tempted Eve to disobey God? And when she did, it caused all the rest of us to have wicked hearts? Well, when Satan saw that Jesus had come to give us new, pure hearts, and to make us good, he thought he would try to stop Him. So he went out into the wilderness to tempt Jesus, as he had tempted Eve in the Garden of Eden.

He came to Him and said, "If you are the Son of God, change these stones into bread, so that you will have food, for you are very hungry."

But Jesus knew why Satan had come, and He refused to turn the stones into bread. He told Satan, "It is written in the Bible that it is better to be hungry than to obey Satan."

Then Satan took Jesus into Jerusalem to a very high part of the Temple. "If you are the Son of God," he said to Him, "throw Yourself down, for it is written in the Bible that the angels will keep You from hurting Yourself."

But Jesus said it was also written in the Bible that we must not put ourselves in danger just to find out whether God will help us.

Then Satan tried again. He took Jesus up on a high mountain and showed Him all the kingdoms of the world at the same time, with their beautiful cities, their mighty armies, and their great riches: and he said to Him, "I will give You all of these if You will only kneel down and worship me." For that is what Satan wanted most of all—to get Jesus to worship and obey him.

But Jesus said, "Get out of here, Satan, for it is written in the Bible,

'You shall worship only the Lord your God, and serve Him alone.' "

Then, when Satan saw that he couldn't make Jesus obey him, he went away; and angels came and cared for Jesus.

Then Jesus returned to the Jordan River where John was baptizing. When John saw Him coming, he said, "Look! There is the Lamb of God!" He called Jesus the Lamb of God because Jesus would die as a sacrifice just as lambs were sacrificed at the Temple. Two of John's dis-ciples heard him say this, and immediately followed Jesus wherever He went. He talked with them, and invited them to His home. Then one of them, Andrew, went to get his brother Peter. The next day two others, Philip and Nathaniel, decided to go with Him. So now Jesus had five disciples.

QUESTIONS
Why did Jesus stay at the Temple?
What did Satan say to Jesus?

46

Jesus' First Miracle

One day Jesus went to the city of Cana to attend a wedding. His mother and His disciples were there too. During the wedding supper something unfortunate happened: the host ran out of wine and the guests would be disappointed. Jesus' mother told Him about it, expecting Him to somehow get some more. Then she told the servants to be sure to do whatever He told them to.

There were six large, stone water jars there in the house, used to store water, for there were no faucets in those days as we have in our homes now.

Jesus told the servants to fill the water jars with water, and they filled them to the brim. Then He said, "Take some to the master of ceremonies." And when they did, the water had become wine!

The master of ceremonies didn't know that Jesus had changed it (but the servants did) so when he had tasted it, it was so good that he called the bridegroom over. "I've never heard of anyone's saving the best wine to the last!" he exclaimed. "Everyone else serves the best first, and after everyone has had enough, then they serve the wine that isn't so good!"

This was Jesus' first miracle. When His disciples saw what had happened, they believed that He was the Son of God.

Jesus' first miracle

47

Jesus Talks with a Jewish Leader

Nicodemus was one of the political leaders of the Jews. After dark one night he came to Jesus and remarked, "Sir, we know God has sent You, for no one could do the miracles You do unless God were with Him."

Jesus replied, "Unless you are born again, you cannot be one of God's children!"

"What?" Nicodemus asked in surprise. "How can a person be born a second time? Can he enter into his mother's body again as a tiny baby and be born again?"

Then Jesus explained to him that by being born again He meant becoming eager to do God's will, and asking Jesus to take away one's sins so that God gives him new, eternal life.

And then Jesus said something else that seems very strange at first. He said, "As Moses lifted up the serpent in the wilderness, so must I be lifted up." What did He mean? Well, do you remember the time when the people of Israel were in the wilderness and God punished them by sending fiery serpents into the camp to bite and kill them? But then God told

Moses to make a bronze statue of a serpent and put it on a pole and lift up the pole so that everyone who had been bitten could look at it; and when they did, they got well.

So now Jesus said to Nicodemus, "As Moses lifted up the serpent in the wilderness, so must I be lifted up." Jesus meant that He was to be lifted up on the cross so that we might look to Him and be forgiven of all our sins. That is, we can thank Him for dying for us.

Jesus also told Nicodemus, "God loves the people of the world so much that He sent His only Son into the world to die for them, so that whoever looks up to Him in faith will not be punished for his sins, but is forgiven and goes to heaven when he dies."

The Jews only offered their sacrifices at the Temple of Jerusalem, but they had churches called synagogues in every city. When Jesus returned to Nazareth, where He had been brought up, He went into the local synagogue on the Sabbath day. He was asked to read aloud to the people from the book of the prophet Isaiah. So He read from the part where Isaiah told

Nicodemus comes to talk with Jesus

the people of Israel about the Saviour who was coming into the world. After he had finished reading and had sat down, everyone in the synagogue was staring at Him. So then He stood up again and preached to them. He told them that what He had just read had come true that very day, right before their eyes. He said that He Himself was the Saviour, the Son of God, whom Isaiah was writing about in the part of the Bible He had just been reading to them.

But when He said this, all the men in the synagogue, or Jewish church, became very angry, for they didn't believe He was telling the truth when He said He was the Saviour. They jumped up and grabbed Him and led Him out to the top of a steep hill on which their city was built, to throw Him off a cliff and kill Him. For they thought it was very wrong for Him to say He was the Son of God. But Jesus walked away from them, and they couldn't seem to stop Him! This was, of course, another miracle.

QUESTION
Do you think Jesus knew how he would die?

48

A Little Sick Boy Is Healed

One day Jesus and His disciples came to the village of Sychar. Just outside the city was a well, called Jacob's Well, where the people came to get water. It was hot, and Jesus was tired from the journey. He sat down by the well while His disciples went into the city to buy food.

A woman came from the city, carrying her empty pitcher to get some water from the well. This woman didn't love God in her heart, and had done many things to displease Him. Jesus knew this, for He sees all our hearts and knows everything we do.

He talked with the woman and told her some of the things she had done that displeased God. She was surprised and said, "Sir, I see You are a prophet." She meant that He must be a person to whom God told things that other people didn't know. "I know that the Saviour is coming into the world," she said to Jesus, "and when He comes He will tell us everything."

Then Jesus told her, "I am the Saviour!"

The woman left her pitcher and hurried back to the village and said to the people, "Come and see a man who told me everything I have ever done! Could this be the Saviour?"

The people rushed out to see Jesus and begged Him to visit their city. So He stayed with them three days, and they listened carefully to what He taught them. Then they said to the woman, "We, too, believe He is the Saviour, but not just because of what you told us about Him; for we have heard Him for ourselves, and we know now that He is the Saviour from heaven."

From that time on, Jesus began to tell the people that the judgment day was coming, and that they must turn away from their sins and trust Him to save them.

He now returned to the village of Cana where He had changed the water into wine. While He was there a rich man from another city came to Him and begged Him to heal his son who was very, very sick. "Come quickly before my child dies," he pleaded.

But Jesus replied, "Go home, your son is already well again!"

The man believed Jesus, so he started back home. But before he arrived, his servants met him and said, "Your son is well!" He asked them what time the child had begun to get better and they replied, "Yesterday at about one o'clock in the afternoon, the fever left him!"

Then the man realized it was the same time that Jesus had said to him, "Your son is well!" So he and all his family believed in Jesus as the Son of God.

QUESTIONS

Why did the lady at the well think that Jesus was the Savior?

How did Jesus heal the little boy?

Jesus talks with the woman at the well

49
Jesus Helps Some Fishermen

Jesus now came to Capernaum, a city beside the Sea of Galilee, and great crowds came down to the beach to hear Him preach. There were so many people that Jesus was almost crowded into the water. So when He noticed two fishing boats pulled up along the shore, with the fishermen mending their nets, Jesus stepped into one of the boats—it belonged to Peter—and asked him to push it out a little way into the water. Then He sat down and taught the people from the boat.

When He had finished, He said to Peter and his brother Andrew, "Now go out into the lake and let down your nets."

Peter answered, "Sir, we fished all night and didn't catch a thing; but if You say so, I'll try it again." And to their surprise, in just a little while they caught so many fish that their net broke! Then they shouted to their partners, James and John, who were in the other boat on the beach, to come and help them, and they filled both boats with fish until they almost sank!

When Peter saw the miracle Jesus had done, he knelt before Him and worshipped. Then Jesus said to Peter and Andrew, "Come with Me." And they left their boats, nets, and everything else, and went with Him everywhere, for now they were His disciples.

On the Sabbath day when Jesus went into the synagogue to teach the people, there was a man there who had an evil spirit in him. The evil spirit screamed at Jesus, "Let us alone; what have we to do with You, Jesus of Nazareth? Have You come to destroy us? I know You—You are the Son of God."

Jesus told the evil spirit, "Be still, and come out of him."

Then the spirit yelled and threw the man down on the ground, and finally came out of him. All the people in the synagogue were astonished and said among themselves, "What kind of a man is this that even the wicked spirits obey Him?"

When they left the synagogue, Jesus went to the home of Andrew and Peter. James and John were there, too; and Peter's mother-in-law, but she was sick, and had a fever. They all begged

Jesus helps the disciples with their fishing

Jesus to heal her. So He went in and stood beside her bed and commanded the fever to leave. Instantly she was well, and got up and cooked dinner for them!

In the evening, at sunset, a great crowd gathered in front of the house, bringing Him many sick people to be healed, and those with evil spirits. And He healed them all, and made the evil spirits come out and go away.

In the morning, getting up long before it was light, Jesus went out to a lonely place in the wilderness to pray. Although He was God's Son, yet He was on the earth as a man who felt pain and hunger, joy and sorrow, and needed to pray for God's help just as the rest of us do. That is why He went out into the desert that morning to pray.

While He was away, many people came to Peter's house looking for Jesus. So Peter and the other disciples went out to find Him, and told Him to come back because everyone was asking where He was. But Jesus replied, "I must go and preach the gospel in other cities, too."

Then He travelled all through Galilee, teaching the Good News in the synagogues and on the beaches. What Good News was it that Jesus preached? It was this: That He had come into the world to be punished for our sins, so that if we turn away from those sins and believe His promise to save us, we won't be punished at the Judgment Day, but God forgives us and takes us to heaven when we die, and we will be happy there forever.

A man with leprosy now came to Jesus and knelt before Him. "Lord, You can heal me if You want to," he pleaded.

Jesus pitied him and put out His hand and touched him. "I want to!" Jesus told him. "Be healed!"

The leprosy left him instantly and he was well again! Jesus told him not to tell anyone who it was who had healed him, but to go to the priest at the Temple and offer a sacrifice, as Moses had commanded those who were cured of leprosy. But as soon as Jesus was gone, the man told everyone what He had done for him!

One special group of Jews were called scribes, and another special group was called the Pharisees. They pretended to be very good, and told the people to obey all the laws in the Scriptures, but they themselves didn't bother with them. They obeyed some of God's commandments, like not working on the Sabbath, but they didn't obey such commandments as being kind and fair. They were hypocrites, that is, they pretended to be good but in their hearts they really weren't at all. So when Jesus told them to turn away from their sins and to obey God, they hated Him and did all they could to keep the people from believing Him.

QUESTIONS

What made Peter and Andrew believe Jesus was the Son of God?

Why did Jesus go out into the wilderness?

What Good News did Jesus preach?

50
Jesus' Twelve Disciples

Now Jesus came again to the city of Capernaum, and great crowds came to the house where He was staying, and He preached to them. The house was a one-story building with a flat roof. Among those who came to Him were four men carrying a sick friend on a stretcher. But there was such a crowd that they couldn't get inside. So they went up on the roof and took off some tiles, and used ropes to let the stretcher down carefully, with their friend on it, right into the room where Jesus was! In fact, the sick man landed right in front of Jesus!

When Jesus saw how much faith they had, He said to the sick man, "Your sins are forgiven!"

But some of the scribes and Pharisees who were sitting there said to themselves, "Who does this man think he is, forgiving sins as though he were God?"

Jesus knew their thoughts and asked them, "Why do you think such sinful thoughts? Is it any harder for Me to forgive this man's sins than to cure him of his sickness? Now I will make him well." Then He said to the sick man, "Stand up and go on home!"

Instantly the man jumped up, stood there for a moment, then picked up the stretcher he had been lying on, and disappeared through the crowd! The people who saw it happen just couldn't get over it. "We've never seen anything like this before," they exclaimed.

In those days the Jews had to pay taxes to the Romans. The taxes were collected by other Jews called publicans and everyone hated them, because most of these tax collectors were unfair—they cheated by collecting extra money for themselves. As Jesus walked along He saw a publican named Matthew sitting at his tax collection booth. Jesus told him, "Follow Me." And Matthew did. He left everything and followed Jesus, and from that time on he was one of Jesus' disciples.

Soon afterwards, Jesus went to Jerusalem to attend the celebration of one of the Jewish holidays, and passed the pool of Bethesda on the way. This pool had five porches around it, all filled with sick, blind, and lame people. Jesus saw a man there who had been sick for thirty-eight years. How Jesus pitied him! This man and all the other sick people had been waiting there because every once in awhile the water moved as if someone had stirred it, and the first person in the water after it stirred was healed of whatever disease he had!

"Do you want to be healed?" Jesus asked him.

"Of course!" the man replied, "But I have no one to help me into the pool after the water stirs; while I am trying to get down into it, someone else steps in ahead of me and I'm too late."

Jesus told him, "Pick up your sleeping mat and start walking!" And immediately the man was well!

But Jesus did this on the Sabbath, the day each week when no work was permitted, so the Jewish leaders scolded the man for "working" by carrying his sleeping mat that day!

"But the man who cured me told me to!" he answered.

"Who said that?" they demanded. He told them it was Jesus. Then the Jews tried to kill Jesus for not obeying their law.

Jesus said that the miracles He did proved that God had sent Him. He told them He was the Son of God and had power to raise the dead—a power only God has. He said the time would come when all who are dead will hear His voice and rise again, and He will judge them. Those who have done good will be rewarded for their obedience, and those who have done evil will be punished for their sins. For His Father has made Him the Judge of all, so that all must worship and obey Jesus just as they worship and obey God.

Another time, again on the Sabbath, Jesus and His disciples were walking through some grain fields. The disciples were hungry, so they picked some grain, rubbed it in their hands to get rid of the husks, and ate the kernels. When the Jewish leaders saw them doing this they again said that the disciples were working on the Sabbath, but Jesus told them it was all right, for God had put Him in charge of the Sabbath, so He knew best about what work could be done on the Sabbath.

On another Sabbath day He went into the Jewish church, or synagogue, and saw a man there with a shrunken hand. The Pharisees watched to see whether Jesus would work on the Sabbath by healing the man! But Jesus knew their thoughts and said to them, "If one of your sheep fell into a well on the Sabbath, wouldn't you pull it out? And if it is right to help a sheep on the Sabbath, how much more a man?"

Then He said to the man, "Reach out your hand!" And when he did, it was healed!

This made the Jewish leaders very angry, and they began to talk about killing Jesus. So He and His disciples left that place and went away to the Sea of Galilee. Many people from Jerusalem and Judea and from countries far away came to see Him when they heard of the wonderful things He did. The sick people crowded around Him to touch Him, for when they did, they got well!

Jesus went alone into the desert and stayed there all night, praying to God. When it was morning, He called His disciples and chose twelve of them to be with Him, and to preach, and do miracles, and to heal the sick and cast

Jesus talks with John and Peter

out devils. These twelve were called "apostles," or "messengers." These were their names:

     Peter,
     Andrew (Peter's brother),
     James,
     John (James' brother),
     Phillip,
     Bartholomew,
     Thomas,
     Matthew (the publican),
     James,
     Thaddeus,
     Simon,
     Judas Iscariot.

QUESTIONS

How did Jesus help the paralyzed man?

What did Jesus tell the Jewish leaders about the Sabbath?

How many of the names of the twelve apostles can you remember?

51

Jesus Talks to the Crowds

When Jesus saw the crowds coming to Him He climbed a hill and sat there with His disciples, teaching them. These are some of the things He told them:

"Blessed are the humble, for the kingdom of heaven belongs to humble people. They are the truly happy ones.

"Blessed are those who mourn, for they shall be comforted.

"Blessed are the meek, for they shall inherit the earth.

"Blessed are those who are anxious to do right and to please God, for they shall be satisfied.

"Blessed are those who are merciful to others, for they shall have mercy shown to them.

"Blessed are the pure in heart, for they shall see God.

"Blessed are the peacemakers (that is those who will not quarrel and who try to keep others from anger and fighting), for they shall be called the children of God."

Jesus told His disciples that when they were treated cruelly because they were His followers, they should be glad, for they would get a big reward in heaven!

He also told them that they must not be afraid to let others know that they loved and obeyed God. Their example would help others to love and obey Him too.

If we do the things God commands, and teach others to do them, we will be great in the kingdom of heaven.

He told His disciples that before they worshipped God and prayed to Him, they must try to remember and set right the wrongs they had done. If they had taken something that didn't belong to them, they must give it back, or if they had told a lie they must confess it and try to catch the lie before it got away any farther. For God won't accept our worship while there is sin in our hearts that we refuse to confess.

Jesus also told His disciples that they must always be pure and good in thought and action; they (and we) must not even think bad thoughts.

And when others are unkind to us, and do us harm, we must not try to pay them back. Instead we must do good to them and pray for them and love them; for then we will truly be the children of our Father in Heaven. We will be like Him, for He is kind even to those who don't obey Him or love Him.

Jesus told His disciples not to just pretend to be nice so that others would praise them for it, but to please God by being *really* nice to others. And when we give help to the poor we must not go around bragging about it.

Jesus said we must not want to be rich, but must send our money on ahead to heaven. How do we do this? By giving our money to the church and Sunday school, and to the missionaries, and to the poor. And then in heaven we will have more things to make us happy than all the money in the world can buy.

This is something else that Jesus said to the people at this time: "You can't obey both God and Satan. For if you obey God you will do what is right, but if you obey Satan you will do what is wrong. So you can't do both—you must choose one or the other.

He told His disciples to stop arguing and blaming each other. This is important for us, too. The person we blame may not have done the thing we blame him for; and if he did, he may not have meant any harm. We can't see his heart and know how he felt while he was doing it; only God knows that, and perhaps God doesn't blame him. And how often we ourselves do the very things we blame others for! Jesus said for us to stop doing wrong before we try to tell others about their faults!

He said that we should treat others as we want them to treat us. If we want them to be kind to us, we must be kind to them.

"Work hard to enter the narrow gate of heaven," Jesus told His disciples, "for the road to hell is wide and smooth." He meant that we must choose the road we will travel along through life. The road to heaven is narrow and rough, where few bother to walk. The road to hell is broad, well-paved, and popular, and stands wide open before us, welcoming us.

Jesus said that not everyone who calls Him Lord and Master will get to heaven, but only those who obey His Father in heaven. Many will come to Him at the Judgment Day and call him "Lord" and will say they have worked for Him and taught others about Him. But He will tell them they have never truly been His disciples. And He will send them away with all the other wicked people because they only pretended to be His disciples but didn't really do what He told them to.

One day Jesus told His disciples an important story about two men who built two houses. One of them chose solid rock to build his house on. When he had finished it, a great storm came up, but the rain and wind could do no harm because the house had such a solid foundation.

The other man built his house on sand, and when the storm came, the rain washed the sand away from beneath his house, and the wind blew against it, and it fell down in a great heap and washed away.

Jesus said that we are either like the wise or foolish man. If we listen to His teaching and do what He tells us to do, then we are like the wise

man who built his house on the rock.
But those who listen to Him but don't
do what He tells them to are like the
foolish man who built his house on
the sand. Those who do what He tells
them to will be saved, but those who
disobey Him will be lost, for the storm
means the Judgment Day.

QUESTIONS
What should we do if someone hurts us?
How should we always use some of our
money?

52

Jesus Defeats Death

In the city of Capernaum there lived a Roman army officer who had a servant he dearly loved, but the servant was very sick and ready to die. When the officer heard that Jesus had come to his city, he asked some of the Jewish leaders to go and find Jesus and beg him to come to the officer's house and heal his servant. So they went and found Jesus and pleaded with Him for help. "This officer is a Roman, not a Jew," they explained, "but he has a deep love for the Jews and has been very kind to us and has even built us a church with his own money."

Jesus started off with them to the officer's house. But before they got there, the officer sent Him this message: "Please don't come! For I'm not good enough to have You in my house. Instead, stop where You are and just say that my servant must get well, and he will! I'm sure the sickness will obey Your orders and go away, just as my soldiers obey me and do whatever I tell them to!"

Jesus was very greatly surprised. "I've never before met even a Jew with this much faith!" He exclaimed. "And I tell you, at the Judgment Day many people of other nations who have faith in Me will be in heaven, while many of the Jews won't, because they don't believe."

So Jesus didn't go to the man's house, but healed the servant while he was far away. And when the officer returned home, he found that the servant was well again!

The next day Jesus went to the city of Nain. Just as He was entering the city gate, He met some people carrying out a dead boy to bury him. He was the only son of his mother, and she was a widow, that is—his father was dead. Many of her friends were with her.

When Jesus saw her, He pitied her. "Don't cry!" He said. Then He stopped the funeral procession and went over to the dead boy and said, "Young man, get up!" And the boy sat up, alive! And Jesus gave him back to his mother!

Everyone was frightened by this amazing miracle, and how they praised God! "Jesus must be a very great prophet indeed to be able to bring someone back to life again," they exclaimed.

One day a man named Simon asked Jesus to come to his home for dinner. But as they were eating, a prostitute* came with an expensive bottle of perfume and knelt at Jesus' feet, crying because she was sorry for her sins and wanted to be forgiven. Her tears fell on Jesus' feet and she wiped them with her long hair and kissed them and poured the perfume over them.

Simon knew this woman was a sinner, and he said to himself, "If Jesus were really God's Son, He would know who this woman is, and how bad she is, and He would send her away."

Jesus knew what the man was thinking and said to him, "Simon, I have something to say to you: Two people owed a man some money. One owed him a lot, and the other owed him only a little. But neither of them had any money to pay him back, so he told them they could forget about it and they didn't have to give him back the money. Tell me now, which of these two men do you suppose will like him best for being so kind to them?"

Simon replied, "I suppose the one who owed him the most."

"Yes," Jesus said, "that is correct." Then He turned to the woman and said to Simon, "Do you see this

woman? When I came into your house, you didn't give Me any water to wash My feet, but she has washed My feet with her tears, and wiped them with her hair. You didn't give Me the customary kiss of greeting on my cheek, but this woman has kissed My feet again and again. And so her many sins are forgiven, for she loves Me so much. But those who have little to be forgiven for will love Me only a little."

Then Jesus turned to the woman and said, "Your sins are forgiven; go home in peace!"

After this Jesus went through the entire country, preaching the Good News in every city and village; and the twelve apostles were with Him.

Jesus was very poor, though He could have been very rich if he had wanted to be, for the world was His. Yet He chose to be poor and to suffer for us so that He could save us from being punished for our sins. And because He was so poor, some of the women He had healed gave Him the things He needed. One of them was named Mary Magdalene, another Joanna, and another Susanna, and there were many others.

---

*Definition for younger readers: "A woman who goes to bed with men she isn't married to." This is strictly against God's laws.

QUESTIONS

Did Jesus go to the army officer's house to heal the servant? Why not?

What miracles did Jesus do for the widow of Nain?

Why didn't Jesus send the prostitute away?

53
Some Parables

Jesus often told the people stories which contained lessons. These stories are called parables. One of His stories made them see how foolish and wicked it was for them to put their trust in money. Here is the story:

"There was a rich man with many farms and orchards. When harvest time came, his crops were so large that his barns wouldn't hold them all. Then he said to himself, 'What shall I do? I haven't enough space to store my harvest. I know! I'll tear down my barns and build larger ones. Then I can eat, drink, and be merry, for I'll be rich enough to live for many years without ever working again.'

"But God said to him, 'Fool! To-night you die! Then who will get all your wealth?'

"All those who live to get rich are like that foolish man. For death often comes when they are least expecting it, and they must leave their money for others, and go away to a world where nothing but sorrow has been stored up for them."

Jesus told His disciples not to be afraid of being poor. "Be like the birds," He said. "They don't plant seeds in the fields, or reap grain, yet they have enough to eat because God feeds them. And God cares more about you than He does about the birds! And look at the flowers! They don't need to work hard to get clothes for themselves, and yet they are more beautifully clothed and have brighter colors than Solomon the king of Israel! So if God gives such beautiful clothing to the flowers, which are of so little value that one day they are growing in the field and the next are cut down and burned, He will surely give you all the clothes you need. So don't be afraid to trust Him. Your heavenly Father knows what you need. The most important thing for you to do is to obey Him and to be His child. Then He will give you everything you need."

Great crowds surrounded Jesus as He walked along the shore of the lake, so He got into a boat and taught the people from there. He told them this story:

"A farmer went out into the field to sow grain. Some of the seed fell on the hard ground of a path that ran along beside the edge of the field, and the birds flew down and ate it. Some of the seed fell on stony places where there wasn't enough earth on top of the rocks to make strong roots, so in a few days the little plants withered away. And some of the seed fell where briars and weeds were growing; the seeds began to grow but the weeds were tall and thick and shut out the sunshine and used up the rain, so the little plants soon died. But the rest of the seed fell on good ground—plowed and harrowed and ready to receive it. The rain watered it, and the sun shone down upon it, and it soon grew; and after a few months there was a harvest of grain—a hundred times as much as the farmer had planted."

When Jesus was alone with His disciples, they asked Him to explain this parable to them. He told them that the seed meant His words. Some of His words are heard by people with hard hearts who refuse to believe Him. Satan comes and takes God's words away from them by making them think of other things, just as the birds ate the seed that fell on the hard pathway. Other people to whom Jesus speaks try for awhile to obey Him, but it is only for a little while. As soon as they have trouble, or are laughed at by others, they turn away from Him. This is like the seed that falls on the stony ground; at first it grows quickly, but in a few days it withers away.

Other people hear Jesus preach and are glad, but afterwards they begin to care more for their homes, their money and their pleasures than they do for the things of God. This is the seed that fell among thorns, and the thorns grew up and choked it.

But there are some people who listen carefully to everything Jesus says, and remember it, and try every day to obey whatever He tells them to. They are like the good soil where the seeds grew well and there was a crop of a hundred times as much seed as the farmer had planted.

QUESTIONS

Why did Jesus say it was foolish to worry about earning lots of money?

In Jesus' story, what happened to the seed?

What did Jesus mean? Do you have good seed in your heart?

54
Miracles!

That evening Jesus and His disciples got into a boat to sail over to the other side of the Sea of Galilee. But suddenly it began to be windy, and soon there was a great storm, and the waves dashed into the boat and began to fill it with water so that it was beginning to sink. But Jesus was asleep.

"Master!" they shouted to Him, "Save us! We'll all be drowned!"

Then Jesus stood up and spoke to the winds and the sea, and said to them, "Peace! Be still!"

The wind stopped blowing, and the sea became very still and calm. Then He said to His disciples, "Why were you afraid? How is it that you have so little faith?"

So they went on to the other side of the lake, and when Jesus got out of the boat, there was a man there with an evil spirit in him. The man had torn off his clothes and was naked and very fierce, so that no one could go by him without getting hurt. His friends had often tied him with chains to keep him at home, but he broke the chains and went out and lived in a graveyard, crying out and cutting himself with stones.

While Jesus was still far out on the lake, the man saw Him and ran to Him as He stepped ashore and fell down at His feet and worshipped Him. The evil spirits in the man were frightened when they saw Jesus, for they knew He could make them go away. They begged Him to let them enter a herd of pigs feeding nearby, and Jesus told them they could. So the evil spirits came out of the man and went into the herd of pigs. Then the whole herd (there were about two thousand of them) ran over to a cliff and tumbled off into the sea, and were drowned.

The men who had been taking care of the pigs ran into the nearby city and told everyone what had happened. So all the people came rushing out to see Jesus. When they saw the wild man sitting there quietly—clothed, and in his right mind—they were afraid, and asked Jesus to go away from their country.

So He got back into the boat to leave. The man begged to go with Him, but Jesus said, "No, go home to your friends and tell them what great things the Lord has done for you." So the man began telling everyone how Jesus had made him well.

QUESTIONS
What happened when the storm came?
How did Jesus heal the man who had evil spirits in him?

Jesus calms the storm

55

Sick People Get Well

As soon as Jesus returned to Capernaum, one of the leaders of the local Jewish church came and knelt at His feet and told Him, "My little daughter is very sick and I'm afraid she is going to die. Oh, please come and put your hands on her head, so that she will get well again."

Jesus went with him, and so did His disciples, followed by a great crowd. In the crowd was a woman who had suffered for twelve years from a disease no doctor could cure; she had given them all the money she had, but was no better—in fact, she was worse. But when she heard that Jesus was in town she said to herself, 'If I can only touch Him, I'll get well.' So she pushed her way through the crowd and touched Him; and as soon as she did, her sickness was cured.

Immediately Jesus turned around to the crowd and asked, "Who touched Me?"

The disciples were disgusted with Him. "Why ask such a foolish question?" they said. "The whole crowd is pushing and touching You!" But He still kept looking around to see who had done it. When the woman saw

that He knew what she had done, she came trembling and fell at His feet, and told all the people why she had touched Him, and how in a moment she was well.

"Daughter, don't be afraid," Jesus said to her. "Because of your faith in Me you are healed."

While He was still talking to the woman, a messenger arrived to tell the little girl's father, "Your child is dead. It's no use for the Master to come now."

But Jesus told the father, "Only have faith and she will come back to life!"

When they arrived at the house, Jesus saw the people weeping and wailing and said to them, "Why weep? The child isn't dead, she is only asleep!" He meant that she would soon be alive again, like one wakened from sleep. But they didn't believe Him, and laughed at Him. Then Jesus told all of them to leave, and took three of His disciples—Peter, James, and John—and the father and the mother of the dead child, and went into the room where she lay. Then He took her by the hand and said, "Get

Jesus brings Jarius' daughter back to life

up, little girl!" And the little girl—she was twelve years old—jumped up and started walking! Then Jesus said to give her something to eat!

As Jesus left her home, two blind men followed Him, calling, "Oh, son of David, have mercy on us." They called Jesus this because He was a relative of King David's, and this was a title of honor and respect among the Jews.

"Do you believe that I am able to make you well?" Jesus asked them.

"Oh, yes, Lord!" they replied. Then He touched their eyes, and immediately they could see.

"Don't tell anyone what I have done for you," Jesus told them, but they told everyone!

Now a man was brought to Him who couldn't talk because of an evil spirit in him. So Jesus told the evil spirit to go away, and it did. Then the man could talk again! "What wonderful things are happening today," all the people exclaimed.

But the Jewish leaders were jealous of Jesus and hated Him. They told the people that He was able to cast out devils only because Satan, the prince of the devils, was inside Him. What a wicked thing to say!

Jesus now returned to Nazareth where He had been brought up, and went into the Jewish church on the Sabbath day and taught the people. They were amazed at His wonderful sermon. "Where did this man get such great wisdom and power to do such wonderful miracles?" they asked. "Isn't He the son of Joseph the carpenter, and of Mary? And aren't His brothers and sisters here with us?"

So they refused to believe He was anything special, because He seemed so common to them. And because they didn't believe, He did few miracles among them except to put His hands on a few sick people to heal them.

QUESTIONS

Jesus said, "Because of your faith in me you are healed." What does it mean to have faith?

Why did Jesus do only a few miracles in his home town?

56

Power for Jesus' Disciples

Jesus now sent His twelve disciples all through the land to preach the Good News. But He told them to go only to the Jews, for they were God's chosen people, and God wanted the Good News preached to them first.

Jesus gave the disciples power to do miracles so that everyone would believe what they preached. "Wherever you go," He told them, "heal the sick, make the lepers well, raise the dead, and tell everyone that Christ has come to save all who believe on Him. But don't expect them to be kind to you! They will treat you as they have treated Me. They will take you before their judges and whip you because you preach to them about Me. But don't fear them, for they can only kill your bodies. Fear God who is able to destroy both soul and body in hell."

Jesus told them not to take any money or food with them on their trip, for God would give them all they needed. "God even cares about the sparrows and feeds them," Jesus said, "and not one of them dies without God's knowing about it. So don't be afraid that He won't take care of you! For you are much more valuable

to Him than the sparrows are! He remembers the smallest thing about you, and knows even the number of hairs on your head. And He will notice everyone who treats you well. When anyone is kind to you, he is being kind to Me, and whoever gives you even a drink of cold water because you are My disciples will be rewarded for doing it."

When Jesus had finished talking to them, they went out to the cities and towns preaching to the people and healing those who were sick.

Afterwards, when they returned, they told Him all they had done. "Let's get away to some quiet place where you can rest awhile," He said. There were so many people coming and going that they scarcely had time to eat. So they all got into a boat and sailed across to the other side of the Sea of Galilee where they could be alone. But when the people saw where they were headed, they followed on foot, walking around the lake to the other side where Jesus was.

As soon as they arrived across the lake the people recognized Him and ran to get those who were sick, so that He could heal them. And where-ever He went, in villages or cities, sick people were laid in the streets and all who touched Him became per-fectly well!

In the evening His apostles came to Him and said, "Send the people away to the villages to buy food, for it will soon be dark."

"They don't need to go away," Jesus said; "you feed them!"

"What?" the disciples exclaimed, "Feed all this crowd?"

"How many loaves of bread do you have?" Jesus asked them. "Go and see."

When they knew, they said, "Five, and two small fish."

He told them to tell all the people to sit down in groups on the green grass. Then He took the five loaves and two fish, looked up to heaven and thanked God for them; then broke the loaves in pieces, and gave them to the apostles; also the two fish. Then the disciples passed them out to the people. And the strangest thing hap-pened! As the disciples broke off pieces of bread, the loaves were still the same size as before, so there was enough for everyone! And it was the same with the fish.

QUESTIONS

Why did Jesus give the disciples power to do miracles?

How do we know how much God cares for us?

What happened to the five loaves and two fish?

57

A Miracle at a Picnic

Jesus now returned to Capernaum again, and went into the Jewish church to teach the people about God.

"What should we do to please God?" the people asked Him.

"Believe that I am the Saviour!" He replied.

But the Jews were expecting a Saviour who would be a great soldier and set them free from the Romans, so that they could have their own king. But Jesus was a poor man, not some great hero. He didn't promise to make them rich, but told them they were sinners. Many people didn't like Him for this, and refused to believe that He was the Saviour, and went away and left Him.

Then He said to the twelve disciples, "Are you too going to leave Me?"

Peter replied, "Lord, where else can we go? For no one else but You can save us."

Then Jesus told them, "I have chosen you twelve to be My apostles, and one of you is My enemy." He meant Judas Iscariot, who was going to help the chief priests and elders of the Jews put Him to death. They hated Jesus and did all they could to keep the people from believing Him.

Jesus then left the country of Israel and went to Tyre and Sidon. The people who lived in those cities were not Jews, but Gentiles. While He was there a woman begged Him to get rid of an evil spirit that was in her daughter. At first He turned away as if unwilling to hear her because she wasn't a Jew, but He did this only to find out whether she truly believed in Him. Then she begged Him more earnestly, and fell at His feet and worshipped Him. "Lord, help me," she begged.

Then Jesus told her, "Because of your faith in Me, your daughter is healed." And when she got home, the evil spirit had gone out of her daughter and she was perfectly well.

Jesus now returned to Israel. A deaf man who could hardly speak was brought to Him to be healed. Jesus led him away from the crowd and put His fingers into the man's ears, and touched his tongue with spit, and looking up to heaven, said, "Be opened!" And immediately the man was well and could both hear and speak!

Soon many sick people who were lame and blind, or couldn't speak, were brought to Him and laid before him so that He could heal them. And He healed them all. The people marvelled as they saw the lame walking, and the blind seeing. And how they thanked God!

QUESTIONS

What kind of Savior were the Jews expecting?

Why did Jesus say that one of the twelve apostles was his enemy?

Can you remember two of the miracles Jesus did?

Five loaves and two fish feed 5,000 people!

58

Who Is Jesus?

As Jesus was going to the city of Caesarea with His twelve disciples, He asked them, "Who do the people think I am?"

"Some say You are John the Baptist, risen from the dead," they answered. "Others say You are the prophet Elijah, come back to earth again."

Then Jesus asked, "Who do you think I am?"

Peter replied, "You are the Christ, the Son of God." In other words, Peter was telling Jesus that he believed He was the Saviour. But Peter and the other disciples were looking for a Saviour who would save them from being ruled by Rome. They knew He was poor, but they expected Him to become rich and great, and believed that He would make them great, too. Like the rest of the Jews, they had not yet learned that He had come to rule in their hearts. Instead of fighting battles for them as a king, He was going to die on the cross for their sins.

Now Jesus began to tell his disciples what was going to happen to Him when He arrived in Jerusalem:

He would be cruelly treated by the chief priests and other leaders of the Jews. In fact, they would kill Him, but He would come back to life again three days afterwards.

When Peter heard this he exclaimed, "No, these things will never happen to You." But it was for this very reason—to suffer these things—that Jesus came into the world. So when Peter said they would not happen to Him, Jesus was displeased and called Peter His enemy. For Peter didn't want Him to do what would please God, but what would please Peter.

One day Jesus took Peter, James, and John up on a high mountain to pray. As He prayed His face began to shine like the sun and His clothing glistened and became as white as snow. Suddenly two men were standing beside Him, talking with Him. They were Moses and Elijah, who had died many hundreds of years before. Now they had returned to this world to talk with Jesus about His being crucified at Jerusalem.

The disciples recognized these two men—we don't know how—and were too excited and frightened to know what to think. Finally Peter exclaimed, "Master, this is great! Would You like us to get three tents—one for You, one for Moses, and one for Elijah?"

But just then a bright cloud came across the sky and God's voice spoke from the cloud. "This is My beloved Son," God called to them. "Listen carefully to everything He tells you."

The disciples fell face downward to the ground in awful fear, but Jesus came and touched them and said, "Get up, don't be afraid." When they stood up and looked around, Moses and Elijah were gone; and no one was there except Jesus. Then Jesus told them, "Don't tell anyone what you have seen until after I have died and become alive again." But they didn't understand what He meant when He spoke of becoming alive again.

When they came down from the mountain the next day, many people were waiting to see Jesus. A man came and knelt before Him and pleaded, "Master, please help my son, my only child. An evil spirit has gotten into him, and it tried to kill him by making him fall into the fire and into the water. I took him to Your disciples, but they couldn't heal him. Oh, please, help me."

"Bring him here," Jesus told him. But as the father was bringing his boy, the evil spirit in the boy threw him to the ground, foaming at the mouth. Jesus asked his father, "How long has he been this way?"

"From the time he was just a little child," the father replied.

Then Jesus said to the evil spirit,

"I command you to come out of this boy and never enter him again!"

Instantly the spirit began shrieking and then came out as the boy lay on the ground, apparently dead. "The evil spirit killed him," everyone said. But Jesus took the boy by the hand and pulled him to his feet, and he was well!

When Jesus and the disciples went back to Capernaum, the tax collectors asked Peter whether or not Jesus was going to pay the Temple tax. Jesus knew the men were talking to Peter about this, so when Peter came back into the room Jesus said to him, "Go to the Sea of Galilee and throw in a hook and a fishing line. Open the mouth of the first fish you catch, and you will find a piece of money in it! Give it to these men as the tax for both of us." So Peter did as Jesus said, and found the piece of money and gave it to the men!

Now although Jesus had plainly told the disciples what was going to happen to Him—that He would be treated cruelly and put to death at Jerusalem—still they never seemed to understand. They thought that even if He had to suffer, soon afterwards He would be crowned the king of Israel and become very great, and then they would be great too!

QUESTIONS

Who did Peter believe that Jesus was?
What did God say to the disciples?
How did Jesus help the little boy?

59

The Good Samaritan

When Jesus arrived in Jerusalem, He went to the Temple to teach the people about God. "Soon I'll be going back to My Father," He told them, "and then you will look for me but won't be able to find Me. And you can't go where I am going because you refuse to believe that I am the Son of God. So you will die without having your sins forgiven. But if anyone believes Me, he will never really die."

Jesus meant that those who trust Him will have eternal life after death. But the Jews thought He was saying that they would never die at all. "Abraham died," they said, "and the prophets died, and yet you say that if a man believes You, he will never die! Are you greater than Abraham and the prophets?"

Jesus replied that Abraham knew about Him and His coming to earth, and believed and trusted Him.

"Of course!" the Jewish leaders sneered. "Why, you aren't even fifty years old—how could you have known Abraham?"

Jesus told them that He had been alive in heaven before Abraham was born. This made them so angry that they picked up stones to throw at Him and kill Him, but He just walked away.

Another day while He was teaching the people, a lawyer asked Him this question: "Master, what must I do to be saved?"

"What does God's law say?" Jesus asked him.

The lawyer replied that the Bible said for him to love God and his neighbors.

"Right!" Jesus replied, "Do that and you will be saved!"

"But who is my neighbor?" the lawyer asked.

Jesus answered by telling him this story: "A man was travelling from Jerusalem to Jericho, but some robbers stopped him and stole his clothing and beat him up. He was seriously wounded, and the robbers left him half dead beside the road. While he lay there on the ground, too weak to get up, a Jewish priest went by. He was a minister and a teacher of God's law, but instead of being kind to the wounded man, he crossed over to the other side of the road and went on, pretending he didn't see the man ly-

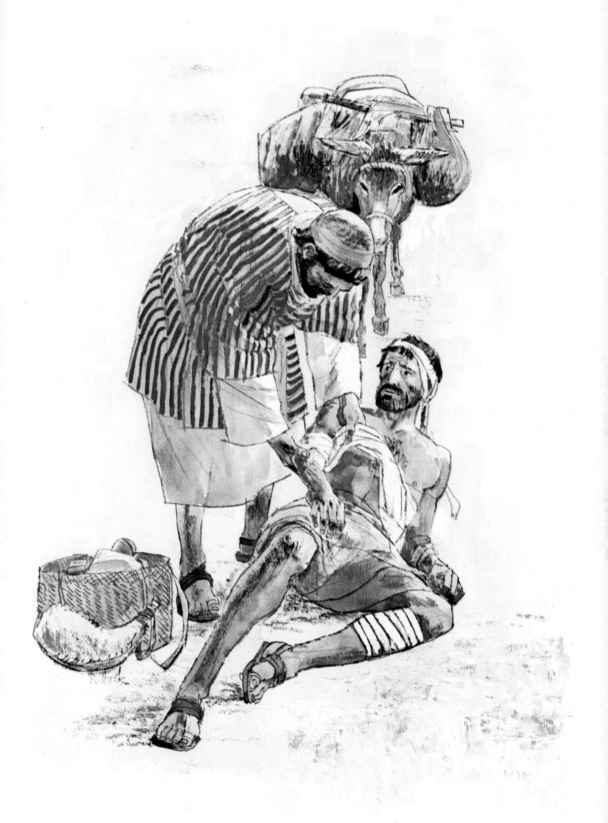

A Samaritan helps the wounded man

ing there. Next, a Levite came along (Levites were the men who helped people worship at the Temple) but when he saw the man, he too went right on without trying to help him.

But then, a Samaritan came by. The Jews hated the Samaritans so it wouldn't be surprising if this Samaritan had refused to help the wounded Jew. But when he saw him he pitied him, and pulling out his first aid kit, bandaged up his wounds, and put medicine on them. Then he helped him onto the back of his donkey, and took him to a hospital, and paid the man's bill.

"Which of these three men was a neighbor to the wounded man?" Jesus asked the lawyer.

"The one who helped him," the lawyer replied.

Then Jesus told him, "Go and do the same to everyone who needs your help." Jesus meant that people who say they love God must prove it by being kind to others.

Jesus now went out to the village of Bethany, a little way from Jerusalem, to visit two sisters named Martha and Mary and their brother Lazarus. When Jesus arrived, Mary sat at His feet to listen to Him tell about the way to heaven. But Martha kept on working in the kitchen and was angry with her sister for not helping. She said to Jesus, "Sir, don't You even care that Mary has left all the work for me to do? Tell her to come and help me."

But Jesus said, "Martha, Martha, you get upset so easily. Only one thing is important and Mary has chosen it.

And I don't think I should tell her not to." Mary had chosen to listen to Jesus, the very most important thing that any of us can ever do.

Jesus now taught His disciples how to pray, giving them this sample prayer: "Our Father in Heaven, may Your name be reverenced by everyone. May Your kingdom come soon. May Your will be done on earth as it is in heaven. Give us this day our daily bread, and forgive us our sins just as we forgive those who sin against us. And lead us not into temptation but deliver us from evil. For Yours is the kingdom, and the power, and the glory forever, Amen."

Now Jesus chose seventy more disciples besides the first twelve, and sent them out two by two into every city and town where He Himself expected to follow later. He told them to heal the sick and to preach the Good News to people everywhere.

Afterwards they returned to Him full of joy because they had been able to do wonderful miracles in His name. But He told them not to be glad just because they had power to do miracles, but because their names are written down among those whose sins are forgiven, and who will go to heaven when they die.

QUESTIONS

What did Jesus mean when he said, "If anyone believes in me, he will never really die"?

What does the story of the Good Samaritan mean?

What important thing did Mary do?

Mary listens to Jesus instead of helping Martha!

60

The Good Shepherd

Another time Jesus said to His disciples, "I am the good shepherd and I know My sheep." He meant that He was like a shepherd to His disciples, and they were like His flock of sheep. In that country the shepherd walked ahead of his sheep, and they followed him. Each sheep had its own name and knew its own shepherd's voice, and came when he called it. The shepherd stayed with his sheep night and day to keep them from being lost, and to guard them from wild animals. Yes, Jesus is our shepherd and is always with us to guard us from Satan and to show us the way to heaven.

Jesus now went again to the Temple, and the Jewish leaders crowded around Him and demanded, "If You are the Son of God, why don't you say so?"

Jesus replied, "I have, but you wouldn't believe Me because you are not My sheep. My sheep listen to My voice and follow Me, and I give them eternal life. They will never be lost —no one can ever take them away from Me. My Father gave them to Me, and no one can kidnap them. My Father and I are One." Jesus meant that He is God—not God the Father, but God the Son. He is as good and as great as God the Father, and He is to be loved and worshipped as such.

Then the Jewish leaders picked up stones to hurl at Him and kill Him because He said He was God, but He escaped from them, left Jerusalem, and went out beyond the Jordan River to the place where John had baptized Him. Crowds came to listen to Him there, and many of them believed Him.

QUESTION
Do you understand how Jesus is like a good shepherd?

The good shepherd

61

Jesus Brings Lazarus Back to Life

About that time Lazarus, Mary and Martha's brother, became ill. His sisters sent a message to Jesus to tell Him about it. Jesus loved Lazarus, Martha, and Mary very much, but when He heard of Lazarus' serious sickness, He didn't go at once to help them, but stayed where He was for two more days.

Then He said to His disciples, "Now, let's go to Bethany, for Lazarus is asleep and I will go and waken him." Jesus meant that Lazarus was dead, and that He was going to bring him back to life again. But His disciples thought He meant Lazarus was resting.

Then Jesus told them plainly, "Lazarus is dead."

Bethany is about two miles away from Jerusalem, and many of the Jewish leaders had gone there to be with Martha and Mary, to try to comfort them in their sorrow. When Martha heard that Jesus had arrived, she went out to meet Him, but Mary stayed in the house.

Martha said to Him, "Sir, if You had been here, my brother wouldn't have died. But I know that even now

whatever You ask of God will be given to You."

Jesus said to her, "Your brother will live again."

"Yes, of course," Martha replied, "—at the Judgment Day."

Then Martha went back to the house and told Mary that Jesus had arrived and wanted to see her. So Mary ran out to where He was, and knelt down at His feet and said, "Lord, if You had been here, my brother wouldn't have died."

When Jesus saw her crying, and the Jewish leaders crying too, He was angry because they didn't think He could help them. "Where have you buried Lazarus?" Jesus asked them.

"Sir, come and see," they replied.

Then Jesus wept.

"See how He loved him," the Jews said. And some of them asked, "Couldn't this man who opens the eyes of blind men have saved Lazarus from dying?"

Lazarus' body had been placed in a cave with a stone rolled across in front of it, to seal it.

"Take away the stone," Jesus said. But Martha objected. "By this time his body has begun to decay," she protested, "for he has been dead four days. The smell will be terrible."

"Didn't I tell you that if you would only believe in Me, you would see how great God's power is?" Jesus asked.

Then they took away the stone and Jesus shouted, "Lazarus, come out!" And he came out, wrapped up in the sheet he had been buried in. "Unwrap him," Jesus told them, and they did.

When the Jewish leaders who had come to visit Martha and Mary saw this great miracle, many of them finally believed on Jesus. But some went to the Pharisees and told them what they had seen.

The Pharisees and chief priests were terribly disturbed and called a meeting to discuss it. "What shall we do?" they said. "There is no arguing with the fact that this man Jesus does wonderful miracles. But if we let him alone, everyone will believe he is God's Son and make him their king; and then the Romans will be angry, and come and destroy our government."

So from then on the Jewish leaders began plotting how to get rid of Him by killing Him.

QUESTIONS
Tell how Jesus helped Lazarus.
Why did the Jewish leaders want to kill Jesus?

62

The Runaway Boy

One day Jesus told them this story: "A man had two sons. The younger one said to him, 'Father, give me my share of the money you are planning to divide up among your sons.' So his father died, and soon afterwards this younger son took the money and went away to a distant country, and spent it all doing all sorts of bad things.

"When the money was gone, there was a great famine in that land, and he began to be very hungry. Then he hired himself out to a man who sent him into his fields to feed pigs. He was so hungry he wanted to eat the husks the pigs ate, but of course he couldn't digest them, so he went hungry instead.

"Finally he said to himself, 'At home even the servants have plenty to eat, while I am here starving. I'll go to my father and tell him, "Father, I have sinned against God and you, and don't deserve to be called your son anymore; just let me be one of your hired servants."'

"So he returned to his father. And while he was still far away, his father saw him and ran out to meet him and threw his arms around him and kissed him. Then his son began his speech: 'Father,' he said, 'I have sinned against God and you, and don't deserve to be called your son any more . . .'

"But his father said to the servants, 'Bring out my best suit for him, and get him some shoes, and go get the finest calf and kill it and let's have a party; for this son of mine was lost and is found.' So they had a big dinner to celebrate his son's return.

"When the older son returned home that evening from working out in the fields, he heard the music and dancing and called one of the servants, and asked him what was going on.

" 'Your brother's back!' the servant told him, 'and your father has killed the best calf for a big party because he is back safe and sound.'

"But the older son was angry and wouldn't go in. His father came out and begged him.

" 'Look,' he told his father, 'I've worked hard for you all my life, and in all that time I've never disobeyed your instructions, yet you never once gave a party for me and my friends. But as soon as this son returns after throwing away your money and doing

The father welcomes his son home

all sorts of bad things, you kill the best calf on the farm for him.'

"The father replied, 'My son, I've always loved you dearly, and everything I have is yours. But it is right that we should be happy, for this brother of yours left us and has come home again; he was lost and is found.' "

By using this story Jesus was telling the proud Jewish leaders—who hated Him for preaching to sinners—that God loved those sinners and was willing to forgive them, and was willing to have them as His children if they would only stop being bad and start obeying Him.

QUESTIONS

What happened when the runaway son came home?

How was the older brother like the Jewish leaders?

63
The Rich Man and the Beggar

Another time He told a story to those who love money and spend their time enjoying themselves instead of obeying God.

"There was a rich man," He said, "who dressed in beautiful clothes, and ate only the best foods. And there was a beggar named Lazarus, who was sick and covered with sores. Because he was so poor he had very little to eat, and his friends carried him to the rich man's gate and left him there to beg for the scraps from the rich man's table. Even the dogs seemed to pity him, for they came and licked his sores.

"The beggar died, and was carried to heaven by the angels. He wasn't poor there, for he ate with Abraham! Then the rich man died too, but he went where the bad people go. There, being punished for his sins, he looked up and saw Abraham and Lazarus far away. 'Father Abraham!' he shouted, 'Have pity on me and send Lazarus to dip the tip of his finger in water to cool my tongue; for I am tormented in these flames.'

"But Abraham said to him, 'Remember that in your lifetime you had everything and Lazarus had nothing, but now he is happy and you are sad. And besides there is a great gulf between us, so no one can come and help you, and you can't come to us.'

"Then the rich man said, 'Then please send Lazarus to my five brothers at home, to tell them to repent and obey God, so that when they die they won't come to this dreadful place.'

"Abraham replied, 'The Bible already tells them that.'

"But the rich man said, 'No, Father Abraham, that isn't enough. But if someone returns from the dead and tells them, then they will surely repent.'

"Abraham replied, 'If they won't listen to what God says to them in the Bible, they won't obey Him even if someone rises from the dead.' (Afterwards Jesus rose from the dead, but even so, few people listened to Him.)

Jesus told still another story to teach His disciples that they should continue to pray, and not be discouraged when prayers aren't answered right away:

"Once there was a wicked judge

who feared neither God nor man, and was very unfair. A poor widow lived in his city, and she kept coming to him and asking him to punish a man who had hurt her. For a while the judge wouldn't listen to her, but afterward he said to himself, 'It's not that I fear God, but this woman bothers me, so I'll do what she asks.'

Then Jesus said, "If that unfair judge did what the widow asked because she asked so often, won't God, who is holy and who loves His children, eventually give them what they pray for, even though it seems for a while as though He isn't listening to them?"

QUESTIONS
What happened to Lazarus and the rich man when they died?
What illustration did Jesus use to teach us to keep on praying even when we don't get an answer right away?

64

Jesus Blesses the Children

Once when some mothers brought their little children to Jesus so he could put His hands on them and bless them, His disciples shooed them away. But Jesus didn't like this. "Let the little children come to Me," He said. "Don't tell them not to, for little children are in the kingdom of heaven." He meant that only those who are humble and loving like little children, will ever get into His kingdom. Then He took the children in His arms and placed His hands on them, and blessed them.

Jesus loves little children

65

A Man Up a Tree

When Jesus arrived in the city of Jericho, on the way to Jerusalem, the usual crowds pushed along behind Him.

In Jericho there was a man named Zacchaeus who was in charge of collecting taxes in that city, and because he cheated so much, he was very rich. As Jesus passed through the streets of the city, Zacchaeus tried to see Him, but couldn't because of the crowd, for he was too short. So he ran on ahead, climbed up into a sycamore tree, and waited for Jesus to pass by.

When Jesus came along the road past the tree, He stopped and looked up into the branches and saw Zacchaeus sitting there. "Come on down, Zacchaeus," Jesus told him, "for I am going to your house for dinner!" So Zacchaeus happily took Jesus with him.

As I have already said, Zacchaeus and the other tax collectors were unfair, cruel men. They forced the people to give them more money than was right. But when Jesus came to Zacchaeus' home, Zacchaeus became very sorry for what he had done. He stood up before all the people and told Jesus that he would stop being unfair, and from then on he would be kind to the poor and would give them half of his money. And if he ever took more money than he should, he would give back four times as much as he had taken.

When Jesus saw that Zacchaeus was sorry and was ready to do whatever Jesus told him to, He said that all of Zacchaeus' sins were forgiven. But the Jewish leaders said Jesus shouldn't eat with a tax collector because he was a sinner. Jesus replied that He had come into the world on purpose to be among sinners, to teach them to repent and to save them from being punished for their sins.

QUESTIONS
How did Jesus heal Bartimaeus?
Why did Zacchaeus climb a tree?

Zacchaeus climbs a tree to see Jesus

66

The First Palm Sunday

Passover was now near (it was a happy time, a little bit like Christmas is to us) and many of the people went to Jerusalem to celebrate it. Everyone wanted to see Jesus, and as they stood around in the courts of the Temple they asked each other, "Do you think He will come?" For the Jewish leaders were saying that if anyone knew where Jesus was, he must tell them so they could have Him arrested and killed.

Six days before the Passover, Jesus came to Bethany where Lazarus lived. Lazarus, you remember, was the man Jesus had brought back to life again after he was dead. People from all over the country knew about Lazarus, and knew that he lived in Bethany, two miles from Jerusalem. So great crowds went there to see him. Then the chief priests decided to arrest and kill Lazarus too, because so many people believed on Jesus after visiting Lazarus; for he told them about his experience of dying, and being brought back to life again by Jesus.

Then Jesus left Bethany to go to Jerusalem. When He had come as far as the Mount of Olives He sent two of His disciples to a nearby village.

"You'll see a colt tied there that has never been ridden," He said. (A colt is a baby horse.) "Untie him, and bring him to me. If anyone asks why you are taking the colt, just say, 'Because the Lord needs him,' and they will let you have him."

The two disciples found the colt just as Jesus had said. And as they were untying him, the owners asked, "What are you doing there, untying that colt?"

"The Lord needs him," the disciples replied. Then the owners let them have the colt for Jesus to ride on. They brought him to Jesus, and the disciples threw their coats across his back and Jesus sat on him.

As He rode the colt toward Jerusalem, a great crowd spread their coats on the road in front of Him, while others cut down branches from the trees and made a green carpet for Him to ride over. They did this to honor Him, for that is what people used to do when a king rode through their streets. Then the crowd surrounding

Him began shouting, "Praise God for sending us a king!"

But Jesus knew they didn't really love Him, and that in a few days they would be shouting, "Crucify Him!"

As He neared Jerusalem He began crying as He thought of all the city's wickedness, and of the sufferings that were coming upon His people. He told His disciples that the enemies of the Jews would come with a great army and besiege the city and destroy it. Every house would be knocked down, so that not one stone would be left standing upon another. All this tragedy would come upon the people of Jerusalem as punishment for killing their Saviour who had come all the way from heaven to help them in His own wonderful way.

Upon His arrival in Jerusalem, Jesus went up to the Temple and began healing the blind and the lame who were brought to Him there. But the Jewish leaders were angry and jealous because some school children who were visiting the Temple began praising Jesus for His wonderful miracles.

That evening He went out to Bethany and slept there. In the morning as He returned to Jerusalem, He was hungry, and noticing a fig tree along the road, He went over to see if there were any figs on it; but there were only leaves. Then He said to the fig tree, "You will never bear fruit."

The next day, as Jesus and His disciples were passing that way again, they saw that the fig tree was dead!

QUESTIONS
How did the crowds honor Jesus as he rode into Jerusalem?
What did Jesus ride on?
Why did Jesus cry?

Jesus rides on a colt

67

An Important Story

Although the Jews had seen Jesus do many miracles, most of them still wouldn't believe that He was the Saviour, for they didn't like Him. Others believed but were afraid to say so, for fear the Jewish leaders wouldn't let them come to church anymore. They were more concerned about being well thought of than they were about pleasing God.

Jesus told the people always to be ready for the Judgment Day because no one knew when it would come. Then He told a story about ten girls at a wedding reception. In that country when a man was married, he brought his bride home after supper, and his friends would go out with their lamps to meet them and welcome them to their new home. That is what these ten girls planned to do. They lit their lamps and were ready, but because the bridegroom and the bride didn't come right away, the girls sat down to wait and fell asleep. Five of them had been wise enough to bring extra oil so that if their lamps went out, they could fill them again. But five were foolish, and didn't have any extra oil.

Around midnight there was a shout, "Here comes the bridegroom! Go out and meet him." Then the girls woke up, but the lamps of five of them had gone out—the five who hadn't brought extra oil along. They said to the other girls, "Please give us some of your oil."

But the others replied, "We don't have enough. Some of the shops are still open—go and buy some."

While they were gone, the bridegroom came, and all those who were ready went in with him to the reception and the door was locked. When the other girls came back they knocked loudly at the door, "Sir, open to us," they called. But the bridegroom refused to let them in.

In this parable the bridegroom means Jesus coming back to earth. The ten girls mean all of us who call ourselves His disciples, and who want to meet Him. Will we be ready? Do we really love Him and obey Him? Or have we forgotten to be ready when He comes?

QUESTION

Why did some of the girls in the story miss the wedding reception?

Some girls forgot to bring enough oil for their lamps

68

The First Communion Service

The Passover day finally came. This was a national Jewish holiday to celebrate the night so long before when the Israelis had escaped from Egypt. The angel of death had killed all the oldest boys in each Egyptian family that night, but he had passed over the houses where there was lamb's blood on the door. It was because the angel passed over them that the celebration was called the Passover.

Each year during the Passover celebration, every Israeli family took a lamb to the Temple and killed it as a sacrifice before the altar. Then the priests burned its fat on the altar, but the rest of the lamb was taken home, where it was roasted, and the family ate it that night, just as the Israelites had done so many hundreds of years before when they left Egypt.

The disciples asked Jesus where they should go to roast and eat the lamb, since Jesus had no home in Jerusalem—or anywhere else.

"Go into Jerusalem," He told them, "and as you enter the city you will see a man carrying a pitcher of water. Follow him into the house where he is going, and say to the man who lives there, 'The Master wants you to show us the room you have prepared for us. He will take you upstairs to a large room all set up for you. Prepare the lamb there, for that is where we will eat it."

The disciples did as Jesus said, and sure enough, they met a man with a pitcher, and he took them to the room Jesus had told them about. There they prepared the lamb.

In the evening Jesus arrived with His other apostles and they all sat down for the supper. "I have wanted very much to eat this Passover supper with you before I die," He told them, "for I will not again eat a lamb that has been sacrificed until I Myself am sacrificed for the sins of the people."

But the apostles didn't understand Him. They didn't know what He was talking about. They still thought He was going to become king of the Jews, and that the time for this was very near.

They began arguing among themselves, as they had before, as to which of them would be greatest in the kingdom. Then Jesus told them, "Here in this world the rulers and the wealthy are the greatest, but with you it is different. For whichever of you is

Jesus washes the disciples' feet

the humblest will be the greatest. The one who wants to be the leader must be the servant of all!"

Then Jesus asked them which was greater, the master who ate at the table, or the servant who waited on him as he ate? They said it was the master. Then Jesus pointed out to them that He was their servant, even though he was their master; and they should serve each other as He served them. Then he demonstrated what He meant:

He got up from the table, wrapped a towel around his waist, poured water into a basin, and began to wash their feet and to wipe them with the towel. When He came to Peter, Peter didn't want Him to do it, for he didn't want Jesus to act like his servant. Jesus told him, "You don't understand now why I am doing it, but you will later."

"No," Peter told Him, "You shall never wash my feet."

Jesus replied, "If I don't, you can't be My disciple!"

"Then, Lord, don't wash just my feet, but my hands and my head too!" Peter exclaimed.

But Jesus told him, "When you have had a bath, it is only necessary to rewash the feet!"

After He had washed their feet and returned to the table again, He said to them, "Do you know what I have done to you? You call Me Master and Lord, and that is correct, for I am. If I, then, your Lord and Master, have washed your feet, you ought to wash each other's feet, for you should follow My example; you should do as I have done to you." He meant that we should help each other at all times.

As they ate the Passover supper Jesus said to them, "One of you sitting here eating with Me will betray Me." He meant that one of his disciples would tell the Jewish leaders where he was, so that they could come and arrest him when the people weren't around to protect Him from them.

The disciples were very much surprised and sad when they heard this. They looked at each other, wondering which one He was talking about. Peter motioned to the disciple sitting next to Jesus to find out who it was that Jesus meant. So he asked Jesus, "Lord, who is it who will do such a terrible thing?"

"It is the one I give this piece of bread to when I have dipped it in the dish," Jesus replied. Then He gave it to Judas Iscariot. After that Satan entered into Judas, and Jesus said to him, "What you are going to do, do quickly."

No one at the table knew what Jesus meant by these words. Some of them thought He was telling Judas to go and buy things they needed, or else to go and give something to the poor. Then Judas went out into the night. After he was gone, Jesus said to them, "I will be with you only a little while longer. Before I leave you, I want to give you this new commandment: *LOVE ONE ANOTHER AS I HAVE LOVED YOU. Everyone will know that you are My disciples by your love for each other.*"

As they were eating, Jesus took a small loaf of bread and blessed it, and broke it apart and gave it to His disciples to eat. "This is My body, broken for you," He told them. He meant that His body was soon to be broken and crucified on the cross as a sacrifice to God for them.

Then He thanked God for the wine

Jesus eats with his disciples for the last time

and gave it to them, and they all drank some of it. "This wine," He said, "is My blood given to God so that He will forgive your sins." For soon His own blood would flow like the blood from the sacrifices at the altar. Then He told His disciples to meet together often, after He was gone, and when they came together they should eat some bread and drink some wine as they had just done, to remember Him until He returns.

This was the first Lord's Supper, or Communion service, or the Breaking of Bread, as we sometimes call it. One of the reasons for doing this is to make us think of how our Saviour was punished on the cross for our sins; and we repent of those sins and determine not to do them again; and we ask the Lord to help us.

As Jesus and His disciples were sitting there at the supper table, Jesus told them not to be sad about His being taken away from them. He was going to heaven, He said, to prepare homes for them. Afterwards He would come back again and take all of us who love Jesus to our new home up there with Him.

Then He looked up to heaven and prayed for His disciples, and for all those who would believe in Him afterwards. He prayed that they would be kept from sin, and would love one another.

QUESTIONS
What did Jesus do to act like a servant?
Why did Judas leave?
What was the new commandment Jesus gave his disciples?

69

Jesus Is Arrested

Jesus and His apostles now sang a hymn together and went out to the Mount of Olives, a short distance from Jerusalem. There they went into a garden called the Garden of Gethsemane.

"Sit here while I go and pray," Jesus told them. Then He went a little distance away and kneeled down and prayed. And now He began to be in terrible anguish as He thought about being punished for our sins and separated from God, for He knew that in a few hours He would be crucified. Great drops of blood fell like sweat from His forehead to the ground.

Jesus prays in the Garden of Gethsemane

Then an angel came to help Him.

When He got up from prayer and went back to His disciples, He found them sleeping. "Asleep?" He asked. "Get up and pray so that you will not be tempted to do wrong." Then He went away and prayed again. When He came back He found them sleeping again. He went away a third time, and when He returned and they were asleep again, He told them, "Get up now, for My betrayer is near."

Judas had been watching when Jesus went to the garden. Because it was night, and because only a few of His followers were with Him, Judas decided that this was the best time to betray his Master. So he went to the Jewish government officials and told them that Jesus was alone with His disciples in the Garden of Gethse-mane. They sent a gang of men with Judas to capture Jesus.

Judas was bringing the men to the garden now, and Jesus knew it, but He didn't run. He waited for them to come because it was the time for Him to die. While He was still talking with His disciples, Judas and the others arrived, carrying swords and clubs and lanterns.

"The one I kiss on the cheek is the man you want," Judas told them. "Grab Him and don't let Him get away."

So Judas came up to Jesus, pretending to be His friend, and greeted Him with a kiss on the cheek, as is still the custom in eastern lands when men meet. Then the men grabbed Jesus and held Him.

"Lord, shall we use the sword?" the

disciples cried out. And Peter drew his sword, and struck a servant of the High Priest, cutting off his ear.

"Put your sword away," Jesus told him. "Don't you realize that I could pray to My Father to send thousands of angels to fight for Me, and save Me from death? But then how could the words of the prophets come true, which say that I am to die for the people?" Then Jesus touched the man's ear and healed it.

Turning to the men holding Him, he asked, "Why the swords and clubs? If I am a thief why didn't you arrest Me in the Temple? I was there every day."

Then all the disciples left Him and ran away into the night.

Jesus was first taken to Caiaphas, who was the High Priest that year. All the Jewish government officials soon gathered at the High Priest's palace and Jesus was brought before them.

Peter had followed Jesus a long way off, hoping no one would recognize him; so now he too came along to the palace, and sat down among the palace servants beside a fire they had built in the courtyard because it was cold.

A servant girl came over to him and said, "You were with Jesus of Galilee!" Peter strongly denied it, and said it wasn't so. Then he went out onto the porch. Just then he heard a rooster crow.

Another servant girl saw him there and said to the others who were standing around, "This fellow was with Jesus of Nazareth!"

Again Peter denied it. "I don't even know the man!" he said.

After a while one of the servants of the High Priest, who was a relative of the man whose ear Peter had cut off, said, "Didn't I see you with Him in the Garden of Gethsemane?"

Peter denied it again. And just then he heard the rooster crow the second time, and Jesus turned around and looked at Peter.

Suddenly Peter remembered Jesus' words, "Before the cock crows twice, you will say three times that you don't even know Me." And he went out and cried bitterly.

The High Priest asked Jesus about His disciples, and about what He was teaching the people.

"Why do you ask?" Jesus replied.

"You already know what I teach, for you have listened to Me in the Temple. Nothing I teach is a secret."

One of the police officers hit Him in the face for saying this. "Is that the way to talk to the High Priest?" he shouted.

"Should you strike a man for telling the truth?" Jesus asked him.

QUESTIONS
What were the disciples doing while Jesus prayed?
Why did Judas kiss Jesus on the cheek?
Why do you think Jesus didn't want Peter to fight the soldiers?
What did Peter do afterwards?

70

Insults to the Son of God!

Early the next morning the men who had arrested Jesus brought Him before the Jewish Supreme Court. There the Jewish officials tried to get people to tell lies about Jesus, but no two of them could keep their stories straight. At last two false witnesses came who declared, "This fellow said, 'I am able to destroy the Temple and build it again in three days.' "

Then the High Priest said, "I demand that You tell us whether You are the Christ, the Son of God."

Jesus answered, "I am. And I tell you this, that you will see Me sitting at the right hand of God, and coming back to earth again in the clouds of heaven."

Then the High Priest tore his clothes and said, "We don't need any

Judas betrays Jesus to the soldiers

more witnesses. You yourselves have heard the wicked thing He said—that he is the Son of God. What should His punishment be?" And everyone shouted, "Kill him."

Then they spat in His face and mocked Him, and when they had blindfolded Him, they struck Him. "Tell us, You Christ, who hit You?" they laughed.

Now they tied Him up, and the entire Supreme Court led Him to Pontius Pilate, the Roman governor. "This man tells the Jews to rebel against the Romans," they lied. "He tells them not to pay taxes to the emperor, and says He is the king of the Jews."

"Are you a king?" Pilate asked Him.

"Yes," Jesus replied, "but My kingdom is not of this world, for if it were, My servants would fight to save Me."

Then Pilate went out and told the Court, "I find nothing wrong with this man."

But they were even more fierce, and yelled out, "Everywhere He goes He starts riots against the government, all the way from Galilee to Jerusalem."

When Pilate heard them speak of Galilee, he decided that since Jesus came from there, he would send Him to Herod, the governor of Galilee, for Herod was in Jerusalem at the time.

Herod was glad for the opportunity of seeing Jesus. He had long wanted to, having heard so much about Him, and he hoped to see Jesus do a miracle for him. Herod asked Jesus many questions, but Jesus remained silent as the High Priests and other Jewish leaders bitterly accused Him of many sins. Herod and his soldiers now made fun of Jesus and mocked Him,

putting a royal purple robe on Him, because He had said he was a king.

Afterwards Herod sent Him back to Pilate again.

Then Pilate called together the Jewish leaders and said to them, "You have accused this man of starting riots, but I find him not guilty. Herod has also found him innocent. There is no reason at all to talk about giving him the death penalty."

Now every year, during the Passover, if any of the Jews were in prison for disobeying the Romans, the Roman governor used to set one of them free, and he let the Jews say which prisoner it should be. He did this to please them, and to make them more willing to let him rule over them.

At this time a Jew named Barabbas was in prison for murder. The people now began shouting to the governor to do as he had always done before and set one of the prisoners free.

"Which one?" Pilate asked, "Barabbas or Jesus?"

While Pilate was speaking with them, his wife sent this message to him: "Don't harm that innocent man. I had a terrible nightmare about Him last night."

The High Priests now persuaded the mob to demand the release of Barabbas.

"Then what shall I do with Jesus?" Pilate asked.

And everyone shouted, "Crucify him."

"But why, what has he done wrong?" Pilate asked.

"Crucify him! Crucify him!" they yelled.

When Pilate saw that he couldn't persuade them to ask him to free Jesus, he took some water and washed his hands while all the people watched, and said, "Don't ever blame me for this innocent man's death."

Then all the Jews answered, "Let the blame be on us and on our children."

But Pilate, by washing his hands, didn't rid himself of the blame. For he knew Jesus was innocent, but wouldn't let Him go free. He was afraid that if he offended the Jews they might want someone else than him to be their governor, and he would lose his job. That is why he gave Jesus to them, to crucify Him.

Before the Romans would crucify anyone they would whip him. He was stripped to the waist, His hands were bound to a low post or pillar in front of Him so as to make Him stoop forward, and while He stood in this way,

He was cruelly beaten with rods or whips until His back was red with blood and open wounds. So now Pilate told his soldiers to whip Jesus in this way.

Afterwards, Pilate's soldiers made fun of Him just as Herod's soldiers had. They put a purple robe on Him and placed a crown of thorns upon His head. Then they bowed before Him, pretending He was their king, and shouted, "Hail, King of the Jews!" And they spat on Him, and struck Him on the head with a stick.

QUESTIONS

Who did Jesus say he was?
Why do you think Pilate let Jesus die?
Why did the people ask for Barabbas to be set free?
Why did the soldiers put a purple robe on Jesus?

71

Jesus Is Killed

Pilate still hoped the Jewish Supreme Court would finally let Jesus go, so he spoke to them again. "Once more, I tell you that I find no fault in Him," he said.

Then he brought Jesus out to them, wearing the crown of thorns and the purple robe. But when the Jewish leaders saw Him, they shouted again, "Crucify him! Crucify him!"

"Take him yourselves, then, and crucify him, for I find no fault in him," Pilate told them.

The Jewish leaders answered, "By our law he ought to die because he says he is the Son of God."

Now Pilate was even more afraid to put Jesus to death.

"Where were you born?" he asked Jesus. But Jesus gave him no reply.

"Do you refuse to speak to me?" Pilate demanded. "Don't you know that I have power to crucify you, and power to let you go?"

"You can only do what God will let you do," Jesus answered.

From that time Pilate tried to set Him free. But Caesar, the emperor of Rome, was a jealous and cruel man and Pilate feared him. When the Jews saw that Pilate wanted to set Jesus free, they screamed out, "You are no friend of Caesar's if you free a man who claims he is a king. How will Caesar like that? What do you think he'll do to you?"

Then Pilate was afraid to let Jesus go, for fear the Jewish leaders would tell Caesar. So he gave Jesus to them to be crucified.

Then Judas Iscariot, the disciple who had betrayed Jesus, was afraid because of what he had done, and brought back to the Jewish leaders the thirty pieces of silver they had paid to him for telling them where Jesus was.. "I have sinned," he said, "for I have betrayed an innocent man."

"So what?" they said. "That's your worry."

Then Judas threw down the thirty pieces of silver on the Temple floor, and went away and hanged himself and died.

The chief priests picked up the money. "It's against the law to put it into the treasury at the Temple," they said, "for it was paid for betraying a man to his death." So they used the money to buy a field where foreigners could be buried, who died while visiting in Jerusalem.

Then the soldiers took the purple robe from Jesus and gave Him His own clothes again, and led Him away to die. Jesus had to carry the heavy wooden cross up a hill outside the city, and when He stumbled, they made a man carry it whose name was Simon, who was coming in from the country. A crowd followed Him out to Skull Hill or Mount Calvary, just outside the city gates, where He was to die.

There they nailed His hands and feet to the cross and crucified Him. Yet in His agony He prayed for them. "Father, forgive them, for they don't know what they are doing," He pleaded. He meant that they didn't know how great their sin was in killing the Son of God, or how fearful their punishment would be. Then they gave Him a mixture of gall and vinegar to drink. This was given to people who were crucified so that they wouldn't feel their awful pain quite so much. But when Jesus had tasted it, He wouldn't drink it, for He was deliberately suffering those pains for all of us. They crucified two thieves with Him, one on His right side and the other on His left.

People who were crucified did not die suddenly; they lived in terrible pain for many hours, sometimes hanging on the cross for days before they died. Jesus was crucified in the morning, but hung in agony until the afternoon, while the soldiers who had crucified Him sat down and watched Him there. They took His clothes and divided them up among themselves, and threw dice for His coat.

Pilate told the soldiers to place this sign on the cross above Jesus' head: JESUS OF NAZARETH, THE KING OF THE JEWS. These words were read by many, for the place where He was crucified was near the city.

The people passing by felt no pity

Jesus is crucified with two thieves

for Him, but mocked Him, saying, "If You are the Son of God, come down from the cross."

And one of the thieves who was crucified with Him said, "If you are the Christ, save yourself and us."

But the other thief said, "Lord, remember me when You come into Your kingdom."

Jesus told him, "Today you will be with Me in Paradise." Jesus meant that the sins of the thief were forgiven, and as soon as he died, even that very day, his real self would go to the happy place where Jesus was going.

Jesus' mother and His disciple John were standing near the cross while Jesus died. Jesus saw them standing there and asked John to take care of His mother, since He was going to die and leave her. From that hour, John took her to his own home

and cared for her just as though she was his own mother.

From twelve o'clock noon until three in the afternoon there was darkness over all the land. God sent the darkness because His son was being killed by wicked men.

About three o'clock, Jesus called out with a loud voice, "My God, why have You forsaken Me?" He said this because God seemed to have turned away from Him, and it was true. For God had turned away from our sins for which Jesus was dying.

When one of the men standing there heard His cry, he ran and got a sponge and filled it with sour wine and held it up on a stick to Jesus' mouth so that He could drink it. Jesus tasted it and then cried out, "It is finished," and bowed His head and died.

At that moment the curtain which hung in the Temple in front of the Holy of Holies was torn in two from top to bottom, and the earth shook, breaking great rocks. (And many people who loved the Lord came back to life, and when Jesus rose from the dead three days later, they came out of the tombs and walked into Jerusalem and were seen by many of their friends!)

When the Roman soldiers who were watching Jesus saw how He died, they were terrified, and one of them said, "Surely this man was the Son of God."

QUESTIONS

Why did Judas kill himself?
Who was crucified with Jesus?
Why was it dark in the middle of the day?
What happened when Jesus died?

72

Jesus Comes Alive Again

The Jewish leaders didn't want Jesus and the two robbers to be hanging on the cross the next day, for it was the Sabbath. So they asked Pilate to tell the soldiers to kill them there on their crosses, so that their bodies could be taken down and buried that day.

Pilate agreed, and told the soldiers to break their legs because this would make them die more quickly. So the soldiers broke the legs of the two thieves, but when they saw that Jesus was already dead, they didn't break his legs but instead they pierced His side with a spear, making blood and water flow out.

There was a garden near the place

The women find that Jesus' tomb is empty

where Jesus was crucified, and in the garden there was a new burial place —a cave carved out of the rock. It belonged to a rich man named Joseph. Joseph was a disciple of Jesus, though he had never told anyone for fear of what people would say. But now after Jesus was dead he went boldly to Pilate and begged for Jesus' body, and Pilate said he could take it down and bury it. So Joseph took Jesus' body down from the cross and wrapped it in a new cloth he had bought, and laid it in the cave and rolled a huge stone across the door.

Meanwhile the Jewish leaders went to Pilate and said, "Sir, while that liar was still alive, He said, 'After three days I will rise again.' Please place a guard for the next three days

at the cave where he is buried, so that His disciples can't come in the night and steal His body, and then tell everyone He has come back to life." So Pilate agreed, and soldiers were sent over to guard the cave so no one could get in and steal Jesus' body.

But during the night the angel of the Lord came down from heaven and rolled back the stone from the cave and sat upon it. His face was as bright as lightning, and his clothes were white as snow. The soldiers trembled for fear and became as weak and helpless as dead men. Then they ran into the city, terrified.

Early the next morning, as it was getting light, Mary Magdalene and the other Mary, and Salome, came to the tomb bringing spices to embalm Him, that is, to help keep His body from changing to dust. "But how can we ever roll away the stone from the door of the cave?" they were wondering; for it was *very* heavy. But when they got there, the stone was pushed aside! They went into the cave and there was an angel in a long white robe!

They were badly frightened, but the angel said to them, "Don't be afraid. Are you looking for Jesus? He isn't here; He has come back to life again! See, that is where His body lay. Now go and tell His disciples that He is alive again and that He will meet them in Galilee."

The women ran from the cave in great fear, and yet with great gladness, and went to tell His disciples what had happened. But as they were running, Jesus met them. "Hello there!" He greeted them. They came and held Him by the feet and worshipped Him. "Don't be afraid," He said, "but tell My brothers—My disciples, including Peter—to go to Galilee, for I will meet them there."

When the women told the disciples what the angel had said, Peter and John ran to the cave to see for themselves. John got there first and stooped down and looked in and saw the linen sheet lying there—the one Joseph had wrapped around Jesus' body—but he didn't go inside. Then Peter arrived and went right in. So then John went in too, and they finally realized that Jesus had come back to life again. Before that they hadn't understood what He meant when He had told them that He would be alive again three days after He died.

Meanwhile some of the guards reported to the Jewish leaders what had happened during the night. The Jewish leaders gave them money to get them to lie about what happened, and to say that His disciples had come during the night while they were asleep and had stolen Jesus' body! (How would the guards know what happened when they were asleep?)

"If the governor hears about it and wants to kill you for sleeping," (for soldiers were killed if they slept on duty), "we will persuade him to pardon you," they promised.

So the soldiers took the money and said what the Jewish leaders told them to. But of course, it was a lie, for they hadn't been asleep at all.

QUESTIONS
Where was Jesus buried?
Why was the cave guarded?
What did the women see when they came to the cave?
What happened to Jesus?

73
Jesus Returns to Heaven

Late that afternoon as two of Jesus' friends were walking along to the village of Emmaus, which was about seven miles from Jerusalem, they were talking to each other about all the strange things that had happened that day. Then Jesus came and walked along with them.

But He looked different, so they didn't recognize Him.

"What are you talking about that makes you so sad?" He asked them.

One of them, whose name was Cleopas, answered, "Are you a stranger here, that you haven't heard all the things that have been happening the last few days?"

"What things?" Jesus asked.

"About Jesus of Nazareth," they replied, "He was a prophet and did great miracles. We thought He was the one who would free Israel from the Romans. But the chief priests and other Jewish leaders crucified Him. And now, early this morning, three days after He was killed, some women who are friends of ours went to the cave where He was buried and came back reporting that His body wasn't there, and that some angels told them He is alive! Some of our men went to

the tomb afterwards and found it was as the women had said: Jesus' body wasn't there!"

Then Jesus reminded them about what the prophets had written concerning Christ—that He would be killed, and afterwards come back to life again. Then Jesus began at the beginning of the Bible and explained all that had been written about Him. But still his two friends didn't recognize Him.

As they neared the village where they lived, He prepared to leave them and go on further. Thinking He was a traveller, they invited Him to spend the night with them, as it was getting late in the day. So He went home with them. As they were eating supper together, Jesus took a small loaf of bread, and after He had thanked God for it, He broke it and gave it to them. But as He did this, suddenly they recognized Him, and just then He disappeared!

Then they said to each other, "Didn't you feel warm inside while He was talking with us out there on the road, explaining what the prophets had said?"

They started back to Jerusalem

and right away found Jesus' disciples and others with them, and told them how they had seen Jesus and talked with Him, and how they had recognized Him as He was breaking the bread at the supper table. And just then, while they were telling about it, Jesus Himself suddenly appeared among them and spoke to them! They were badly frightened, for they thought He was a ghost.

Then He said to them, "Look at the nail marks in My hands and My feet. Touch Me and see that it is I, Myself, for a ghost doesn't have flesh and bones as you see that I have!" They could hardly believe it for joy! Then He asked them for food and they watched Him as He ate it. Then He explained to them the Scriptures that told of His dying for the people, and coming back to life again. And now at last, although they had read those parts of the Bible before, they finally understood them.

One of the disciples, whose name was Thomas, wasn't there that evening, so he didn't get to see Jesus. The others told him about it afterwards.

But Thomas replied, "Unless I see the spear wound in His side, I won't believe it was He."

Eight days later as the disciples were meeting together behind locked doors, and Thomas was with them too, suddenly Jesus was standing there among them, and greeted them! Then He said to Thomas, "Poke your finger into the wounds in My hands and thrust your hand into My side, and believe!"

When Thomas heard His voice and realized it was Jesus, he exclaimed, "My Lord and my God!"

"Thomas," Jesus said to him, "you wouldn't believe until you saw Me; but blessed are those who believe even though they haven't seen Me."

A few days later Jesus appeared to His disciples on the shore of the Sea of Galilee. This is the way it happened: Peter, Thomas, Nathaniel, James, John, and two other disciples were there, and when Peter said he was going out to fish, they said they would go along. They did, but caught nothing all night. In the early morning, Jesus was standing on the shore, but the disciples didn't recognize Him.

"Did you catch any fish?" He asked them.

"No," they replied.

"Throw your net out on the right-hand side of the boat and you'll catch plenty of them!" Jesus told them.

They did, and now they couldn't drag the net into the boat, it was so full of fish!

John said to Peter, "It must be the Lord standing there on the shore!" When Peter heard that, he fastened his fisherman's coat around him and jumped into the water to get to shore faster. The other disciples came in the boat, dragging the net. As soon as they came to land, they saw a fire burning, and fish laid on it, and bread.

Jesus said to them, "Bring some of the fish you have caught." Then Peter pulled the net ashore and it was full of huge fish, more than one hundred and fifty of them, but though there were so many, the net wasn't broken.

"Come and have some breakfast," Jesus called. They were almost sure it was the Lord, but didn't want to ask Him! (By this time He had shown Himself to them on several occasions since He came back to life again.)

Another time He met them on a mountain in Galilee where He had told them to go, and when they saw Him they worshipped Him. He said to them, "God has given Me all power in heaven and on earth. Go and preach the Good News to the people of every nation, baptizing them in the name of the Father, the Son, and the Holy Spirit, and teaching them to do everything I have commanded you."

Jesus showed Himself not only to His disciples, but to more than five hundred others at one time.

Forty days after He came back to life, Jesus appeared to the disciples at Jerusalem again.

Then He walked with them to a place near the village of Bethany (where Mary, Martha and Lazarus lived) and blessed them. And while He was blessing them, He began to rise into the air until He disappeared into a cloud!

While the disciples stood there

Jesus is alive and talking with his friends

straining their eyes for another glimpse, two angels appeared, dressed in brilliant white, and said to them, "Why stand here looking at the sky? Jesus will return again someday, just as you have seen Him go!"

QUESTIONS

. When did Jesus' friends recognize him?
· What made Thomas believe Jesus was alive?

Do you remember what the Good News was that the disciples were told to preach?
How many people saw Jesus after he had come back to life?
What happened forty days later?
Have you ever met Jesus? Have you invited him into your heart?

Jesus is taken back to heaven